25
stupid
mistakes
couples
make

also by Paul Coleman

How to Say It to Your Kids

The 30 Secrets of Happily Married Couples

The Forgiving Marriage

25
stupid
mistakes
couples
make

Paul Coleman, Psy.D.

Contemporary Books

*Chicago New York San Francisco Lisbon London Madrid Mexico City
Milan New Delhi San Juan Seoul Singapore Sydney Toronto*

Contemporary Books

A Division of The **McGraw·Hill** *Companies*

1 2 3 4 5 6 7 8 9 0   DOH/DOH   0 9 8 7 6 5 4 3 2 1

ISBN 0-7373-0575-4

Library of Congress Control Number 00-134055

This book was set in Adobe Minion
Printed and bound by R.R. Donnelley & Sons Co.

Interior design by Anna Christian

McGraw-Hill books are available at special quantity discounts to use as premiums and sales promotions, or for use in corporate training programs. For more information, please write to the Director of Special Sales, Professional Publishing, McGraw-Hill, Two Penn Plaza, New York, NY 10121-2298. Or contact your local bookstore.

This book is printed on acid-free paper.

For my parents,
George and Frances Coleman,
who showed me just how sacred
a marriage can be.

And to my beloved wife, Jody,
and our children, Luke, Anna, and Julia.

contents

introduction

Are you happy in your relationship? Do you feel cherished? Or has the love of your life drained the life out of your love?

As a relationship therapist, I've sat with couples for almost 20,000 hours. I've seen what makes relationships flourish and what makes them fizzle. When a couple struggles to keep their relationship afloat, basically two things are happening:

1. Each partner is focusing less on their role in the problem and more on their mate's role.
2. Mistakes are being made—mistakes that are predictable, common, and preventable, but which are happening *repeatedly* anyway.

I can't do much about helping you to look inward and to take responsibility for your share of relationship problems. You'll have to do that on your own. (And if you don't, the relationship will not—*cannot*—become satisfying.) But in this book, I will point out mistakes you have probably made—some severe, some not too severe (some surprising)—and give you guidelines on how to overcome them. My guess is that you've never fully recognized many of the mistakes you will read about here. Ignorance is not always bliss. Other mistakes you will recognize immediately but will have to admit, if you're honest, that you haven't really tried to correct.

PART ONE
mistakes of the mind

1

living together will be the true test of our relationship

Carl and Linda had been living together happily for a year. Happily except for the fact that Linda wanted to get married and Carl did not. "I do not need a piece of paper to tell me I'm committed to you," Carl said.

"But if marriage is just a piece of paper to you, why not get married anyway? What's the big deal?" Linda asked.

Carl's answer never satisfied her. "Wouldn't you rather know that I am staying with you because I *want* to, not because I'm legally obligated?"

Jay and Cindy lived together before marriage but for different reasons. They wanted their marriage—if they should ever decide to get married—to be a success. They didn't want it to end in divorce, as their parents' marriages had. "We care too much about marriage to go into it blindly," Cindy said. "We need to test the waters and make sure marriage is the right course of action."

These were smart couples. And they were making a huge mistake. Linda had strong reasons to question Carl's commitment to her. After all, he did not want to commit to her in marriage. But she stayed with him anyway. Jay and Cindy felt a hopeful sense of commitment. They just wanted to be sure that their marriage would be a success. Their logic made sense to them. But they were making a potential costly mistake of the mind.

✧ playing house is not the real thing

Since 1960, there has been a 700 percent increase in cohabitation among couples. (Slightly over half of all couples live together before marriage.) Thirty years ago, many relationship experts heralded cohabitation as a wise course of action, a decision that freed couples from society's old-fashioned, imperfect traditions. It was a lifestyle choice that promised to automatically improve the quality of future marriages because cohabiting couples who discovered they couldn't get along would break up before they made it to the altar. The divorce rate would plummet. Marital satisfaction would soar. Right? *Wrong!*

The divorce rate has soared along with the rate of cohabitation. And while it is certainly possible that a couple who tests the relationship waters by living together will wind up happily and forever married, the odds are against that happening. Couples who cohabit before marriage have a divorce rate that is one and a half to two times higher than couples who do not cohabit before marriage. Researchers call this the "cohabitation effect."

Compared to married couples, cohabiting couples are less satisfied with their relationship, less committed, and have more relationship problems. A recent study in the *Journal of Marriage and the Family* revealed that cohabiting couples were about as sexually exclusive as couples who dated—in other words, infidelity was much higher in cohabiting couples than in married couples. Alcoholism, infidelity, and drug abuse were the top three problems faced by married couples who had lived together before marriage, compared with married couples who did not cohabit. Cohabiting does not necessarily improve mate selection or future marital quality.

Interestingly, individuals who divorce but who had previously cohabited with their partner are much more likely to cohabit with their next partner. In half of those cases, they bring children along. Thirty percent of childless couples who cohabit have children together while remaining unmarried. Their mistake continues.

Despite the statistics, attitudes aren't changing. In a survey of young adults ages seventeen to twenty-three, most people felt that people should not marry unless they intended to remain together for life. Sounds good so far. But half believed that cohabiting was therefore a good and necessary idea. Eighty percent saw no problem with bearing a child outside of marriage.

In a recent study at Rutgers University, young adults under the age of thirty wanted "sex without strings . . . relationships without rings." Most of these younger people feared that marriages don't last (their parents' marriages didn't last) and that a divorce leads to economic hardship. (Divorce does have a ripple effect. It increases the odds that children of divorce will get divorced, and their children will divorce, and so on.)

Anatomy of Cohabitation

Susan was very careful about selecting a mate. She had been divorced and had two children, both under ten. She didn't want to put her kids through another divorce. But when she met Gary, her concerns started to melt. Gary was a wonderful, warmhearted guy. When their relationship became sexual, Susan was adamant that her children not be aware of it. She'd stay with Gary on weekends when the children were with their father. Once in a while Gary would come to her house late at night, after the kids were asleep, and leave before they awoke the next morning. Soon, she wanted her children to meet Gary. She was growing more certain that she and Gary would eventually marry.

The kids liked Gary. It created awkward moments as they sometimes felt disloyal to their father, but basically the group got along.

Gary's apartment lease was ending soon. Wouldn't it make more sense to live together? They had fallen in love, the kids were comfortable with Gary's presence, and their goal was to get married—some day.

Within two months Gary moved in. Susan and Gary knew that if this test proved itself, marriage was inevitable. Sounded reasonable, right?

Ted and Leslie graduated from college two years ago and each had exciting jobs. Neither wanted to get married until they had established themselves in their careers, a process they expected would take five more years. They purchased a condo, practiced birth control, and were willing to wait a few years before the word *marriage* ever entered their conversations. Sounds mature and practical, right?

REASONS FOR BREAKUP

Susan, Gary, Leslie, and Ted are like many cohabiting couples. While their future marriages may succeed, the odds are they will fail. Actually, there is a 40 percent chance they will break up before they marry. What are some of the possible reasons?

Commitment is low. They may *feel* committed but are unwilling to make that commitment. Their commitment is based more on current satisfaction and enthusiasm than on deep devotion or behavioral standard. This low-level commitment is a pebble in the shoe that can cause much pain. Diminished commitment creates a degree of mistrust over time. Often, one partner is more interested in marriage than the other, causing disagreement and conflict. Such conflict can further raise doubts as to their compatibility and may result in a further delay of marriage.

Rules are fuzzy. If a cohabiting partner wants to purchase an expensive item, does the other have a say? Should the other help pay for it? If a guy wants to spend a weekend with his buddies, should he discuss it with his mate and be open to her views? Or should he just go and do what he wants? If one gets a great job offer out of state, should it be turned down? Should the other agree to go? If the roof needs replacing, who pays for it? The owner, the live-in, or both?

Money is often kept separately. Typically, basic monthly bills are split. Each makes their own car payments, investments, etc. If they have a joint checking account, it is usually small. This has the effect of strengthening each person's sense of individualism at the expense of couplehood. Personal wants and needs usually take precedence over the partner's wants and needs.

Children are present about 40 percent of the time in cohabiting relationships. Stepfamilies typically have more problems to deal with than biological families. But if the partners are unmarried, the non-parent has even less authority over children. Issues of discipline and the cost of raising children can become divisive.

Former relationships are more of a threat. If an ex-girlfriend is in town or if she starts calling and leaving messages, doubts are raised. After all, there is no legal or moral obligation for the man to remain faithful. (In fact, infidelity is the number-two problem for cohabiting couples.) While marriage is no guarantee of fidelity, the truth remains that infidelity is far less of a problem for married couples than unmarried, cohabiting couples.

The vision of the relationship is unclear. Because these couples are testing their compatibility, they stop short of dreaming dreams that committed couples endeavor to make come true. They dream in terms of "maybe." Maybe they'll have kids, maybe they'll have a brother or sister for the child they already have, and maybe they'll buy a big house. Maybe they'll start an IRA. Maybe one of them can return to school to learn a new career. Maybe. They put their lives in a holding pattern while time is running by.

What's a Couple to Do?

Research shows that living together may not harm a relationship *if the couple has clear plans to marry soon.* There seems to be no research showing that living together boosts future marital satisfaction. The best you can expect is that living together may cause no harm.

If you are living together now or plan to cohabit, the best advice is this: reconsider.

The fact remains that it simply is not true that living together will help you improve your chances of marital success. In fact, it will drastically lower your chances. A wise course of action is to presume that your intent to live together (unless your marriage is pending) is already a sign that relationship or personal problems are being overlooked or minimized. Your best bet is to address those problems squarely while living apart. If one of you already has children, *absolutely* consider living apart.

Learning to delay gratification is a sign of maturity and a sign of future happiness. That is true for children, teens, and adults. Studies show that once a teenager experiments with sex or drugs or alcohol, the lid is off. The longer a teen can delay such activities, the better his chances of staying out of trouble and being more successful in school. So it is also with cohabiting. The longer you delay living together before marriage, the better the odds that cohabitation will have a minimal, negative effect.

If your partner is committed to you, he or she will understand if you have misgivings about cohabiting and agree to live separately.

How to Make Your Relationship Last

Okay, you've read this far in the chapter. You may not like what you've read, but hopefully you're intrigued. Most of your friends see no problem with cohabiting,

If you have misgivings about living together, but your partner is pressuring you to do it anyway, your partner may be more committed to a lifestyle than to you.

and until now maybe you saw no problem with it, either. Now what do you do? What personal or relationship issues should you and your partner examine and fix *before* you even consider living together. The key ones are listed below:

BE WARY OF SOME KEY ISSUES

Too independent. If one of you doesn't want to be "tied down," that should be a signal to move on and find someone else, or at least proceed with caution. A low-level commitment by a lover is just that—an inability to promise that this person will stick around. The longer you remain together without getting married, the less likely it is you will get married.

Afraid of divorce. This is typical for people who have experienced a divorce firsthand, either as children watching their parents split, or as adults seeing their marriage dissolve. Children of divorce are less adept at resolving conflict because they had no good role models. If you know that problem-solving skills are lacking, see a counselor or take a relationship enrichment course. Don't live together and "wing it." If you are previously divorced and don't want to get burned again, you must examine your role in the relationship failure. Identifying your ex's defects is no help if you cannot identify your own. Need help figuring out your flaws? Ask your ex, ask your kids, and ask three or more trusted friends or family members.

Too dependent. Maybe you're lonely and have been single too long. Maybe your finances are in ruin and it would be great to have someone with whom to share expenses. Your dependency can interfere with your relationship success. Your partner may want to be wanted but may grow weary if your dependency becomes smothering. If you cannot be complete without living with this person, seek a counselor. Your esteem is too low and you'll be living together for the wrong reason. Your lover should not be throwing you a life preserver. If you need money, continue to live sparsely, find a better job, or borrow. It might be hard, but it is much better to delay financial gratification now and have a better chance of relationship success later. If you are the partner with the money who wants to bail out the love of your life, *wait.* When there is no marriage commitment, any sort of financial obligation can weigh down a relationship. You will feel owed. The relationship will be lopsided.

Disagree about values and goals. A young woman recently came to me and discussed her pending marriage. She and her future husband disagreed about whether to have children. I told her to postpone the wedding. If you disagree about values (the role of religion or spirituality in your life, discipline of children, work versus family, etc.), the place and time to hash out these differences is before you commit to one another. Discovering each other's goals and values is best done while dating, not while setting up a household.

Have young children. For the children's sake, don't live together to see if the relationship will work. Otherwise, the odds are almost certain that your children will endure another relationship loss.

The divorce rate for second marriages is already 60 percent—higher if stepchildren are living with the couple. Don't raise that percentage further by living together. Some states are now giving legal visitation rights to non-parents, if that adult had taken on a role as a "psychological parent" by virtue of sleeping with the

Kids need parents committed to the new family, not those who are simply giving it a test-drive.

children's father or mother and living with the children. Theoretically, all of your live-ins could one day claim rights to visitation. (Then who'll get the kids on Thanksgiving?)

Living together before marriage is almost as common as sex before marriage. But, when living together doesn't work out or when it doesn't add to the success of a future marriage, people still don't abandon the practice. Instead, they've intensified it. They view marriage as the risk and cohabitation as the safety net. But they are wrong. Marriage is far less risky when couples don't live together before marriage.

2
you did that on purpose!

Meg walked through the kitchen after a hard day at work and immediately noticed two things. The adorable new puppy had left its calling card smack in the middle of the floor, and her adorable husband, Ralph, who had arrived home before she did, was reading the mail, blissfully unaware of the puppy's creative pursuits. *Or was he?*

Had Meg and Ralph's relationship been satisfying, Meg would have given Ralph the benefit of the doubt. *Maybe he did miss seeing it. Or, maybe it wasn't there until twenty seconds ago.* But Meg had been feeling unappreciated in the relationship for months. Ralph was less romantic, more interested in his personal pursuits. So her comment today was not brimming with understanding.

"Ralph, why can't you pay attention around here? Why do I have to be the one to clean up after the dog? You're not a child, you know."

∾ give your partner
the benefit of the doubt

Imagine (it's not hard) that your mate is in a grumpy mood. Maybe he's been more distant of late, more interested in his computer or favorite baseball team than in you. Maybe he's been a little too quick to criticize or he easily snaps at the kids. Would you think something like this:

> Gee, maybe his boss is getting to him again.
> I wonder if he's coming down with a cold?
> I know he's been tired lately, more than I realized.
> I wonder what's bothering him?

Or, would something like this run through your mind:

> Just because he's in a bad mood doesn't give
>   him the right to be mean to everyone else!
> He's so self-absorbed. Doesn't he think of
>   anyone but himself?
> Oh, great. Just what I needed. Another kid to
>   take care of.
> I don't care what's bothering him. I wish he'd
>   leave for the day.

If most of your answers fit the first list, it means you are likely to give your mate the benefit of the doubt when difficulties or bad moods arise. You are also feeling fairly satisfied with your relationship.

Giving the benefit of the doubt does not mean you make excuses for obnoxious or repeatedly hurtful behavior. To do so would encourage more obnoxious behavior and would be a sign of low self-esteem and perhaps deep-seated fear. But our beloved mates (unlike ourselves) will occasionally be unkind, forgetful, irritable, selfish, and downright ornery. It can be helpful then to cut them some slack, to look for extenuating reasons for their actions, or to accept their minor faults and be forgiving. That doesn't mean you can't speak up. It's okay to say, "Mike, it's obvious something is bothering you. I'm willing to hear about it if you want to talk, but please stop acting so cranky." If said with concern, not contempt, and if your relationship is reasonably satisfying, Mike will probably cooperate.

Fix the Problem Before It Gets Worse: Five Mistakes to Avoid

Most couples understand that uncooperative, nasty behavior will sooner or later be responded to with uncooperative and nasty behavior—or at least withdrawal. But many couples don't realize that once a person's attitude and expectations have been negatively tainted, it colors all of their perceptions about their partner and is hard to reverse. They become more and more negative, even when there's no reason to be negative. It's as if they were wearing blue-tinted glasses and their mate held up a lemon. The blue and yellow would combine to make the color green.

Dissatisfied partners don't give the benefit of the doubt. Instead, they doubt the benefits of their partner.

"You're holding up a lime."

"No, it's a lemon."

"It is not! Anyone can see it's a lime!"

Truth becomes harder to see because each side thinks they are right. If you are often angry at your mate and view him in an unfavorable light, you will tend to overreact to his undesirable behaviors and underreact when he is considerate. The opposite is true when you and your mate get along well most of the time.

There are five common types of misperceptions when a relationship has gone sour.

BLAME

Distressed couples blame their partners for difficulties and view any negative act as intentional and selfishly motivated. They say and think things such as:

> You did that on purpose!
> You don't care about me, only yourself!
> There you go again. How I continue to put up
>   with you is beyond me!

In contrast, happier couples are able to own up to their own faults and see a partner's negative behavior as unintended, a minor flaw, or due to extenuating circumstances. They say things such as:

> She must be having a hard day.
> He must be worried about his father's health.
> She must have misunderstood me.
> He can be a pain in the ass sometimes, but I still
>   love him.

BAD FAITH

Distressed couples view positive actions by their partners as exceptions to the rule or due to extenuating circumstances. They say things such as:

> Well, it's about time you did something nice for
>   a change.
> Will wonders never cease?
> How come you're not in a bad mood like you
>   usually are? Did you win some money
>   playing cards?

In contrast, happy couples view positive actions by their partner as par for the course. They appreciate it and attribute it to their partner's character.

> He's so thoughtful.
> I married a wonderful person.
> I'm lucky to have found her.

CHAGRIN

In unhappy relationships, even neutral actions can be viewed negatively.

For example: A live-in lover pours himself a cup of coffee. An unhappy partner thinks:

> Oh, sure. He never forgets his morning coffee,
>   but he forgets to call me during the day.

A wife talks on the phone with her sister. A dissatisfied husband thinks:

> She has time for everyone else but me.

In contrast, happy couples view neutral actions as neutral or slightly positive.

> Gee, that coffee looks good. I think I'll have some.
> Oh, good. She's getting a chance to talk to her sister.

REJECTION

Dissatisfied partners (especially women, according to research) will respond negatively when their man tries to show empathy or support after an argument—thereby killing an opportunity to get the relationship on track. They say things such as:

> Forget it. It's too late now.
> Oh, are you trying to show you actually care?
> It's about time.

In contrast, happier women respond positively when their man tries to show empathy or support after an argument.

Thanks, that means a lot.
I knew we couldn't stay mad for long.
I still love you.

PROJECTION

Dissatisfied partners will *imagine* that their partner will respond negatively in some future interaction. They then get angry and act as if their mate actually did respond that way, even though the event never happened.

Man driving home from work: *I'd love to go skiing this weekend, but I know she'll just say no. How did I end up with such a woman?*

Woman driving home from work: *He'll come home late again. He'll blame it on traffic, but he's probably chatting away with the new secretary.*

In contrast, a happy partner may anticipate a partner's negative response but will not make a snap judgment. More likely, she will anticipate something pleasurable.

When your attitude and expectations are negative, your partner could jump through hoops for you but your attitude might not change. Remember that one of the mind traps is to dismiss anything positive as insufficient or to view your partner's motives as less than sincere. Your partner would have to act much more positively for an extended time before it would please you. (Chances are he or she will get discouraged long before that.) Instead, you have to think differently. Your job isn't to pretend your mate is wonderful when he or she is being obnoxious. Your job is to really try to examine any extenuating circumstances, and consider alternative reasons for undesirable behaviors—reasons that don't paint your partner in such an unfavorable light.

> *Whenever you say or do something nasty, don't you explain it to yourself in a manner that doesn't make you seem like such a bad person? Can you give your mate the same consideration?*

How to Halt the Self-Defeating Cycle: Five Mind Shifts for Negative Attitudes

Negative viewpoints are not always inaccurate. Still, even when a partner is objectively in the wrong, it's okay to complain but not okay to question his character. Why? Because our underlying attitudes become self-fulfilling. Negative attitudes provoke negative actions that in turn cultivate more negative attitudes. Conversely, if you respond kindly to a mate's thoughtfulness, they will likely continue to act thoughtfully and your positive view will be strengthened. But if you respond with snide remarks or ignore positive actions, they may stop altogether, thereby confirming your negative outlook.

Trying to give your partner the benefit of the doubt may not be easy if your relationship has been strained, especially when there is a buildup of hurt feelings and ill will. And, chances are, if you try to give the benefit of the doubt, they won't change any of their difficult ways, at least not right away. So you must be prepared to hang in there.

There are five "mind shifts" that can help you look more kindly at your partner when he or she aggravates you. If your partner is abusive, is a raging alcoholic or addict, or repeatedly acts in ways that are immoral or unacceptable, forget about giving him or her the benefit of the doubt. That would be enabling. But if you and your mate are like the typical couple who sometimes gets trapped in a negative spiral of crankiness and selfishness, these mind shifts will reverse the direction of the slide.

RECOGNIZE OLD PATTERNS OF COPING

As a child, your mate may have coped with stress or threats by lashing out or by withdrawing. It is really a fear-based response that is still being relied upon as an adult. For example, if your partner withdrew from conflict as a child, he might disconnect from you when you are upset. But that may only increase your frustration and prompt him to withdraw even further. Or, your partner may have learned from his parents to act in certain ways that you find frustrating. For example, some happy families are loud, quick to criticize, and yet seem to thrive on this "in-your-face" style. If your partner acts that way, he may have no idea of how aversive it is to you. He'll wonder why you hold grudges when he lets things roll off his back. Some children grow up having to take on many responsibilities such as routinely caring for younger siblings. As adults, they may continue that tendency to "take charge," a style that might irritate a mate. Oldest children often like to get their way. Partners who both were the eldest in their family might butt heads more often. Modifying these patterns may be necessary.

CONSIDER THAT YOUR MATE IS FRUSTRATED, NOT MEAN

When frustrations and misunderstandings accumulate, mates sometimes say hurtful things as a way to call attention to the fact that they are hurt, angry, overwhelmed, or at a complete loss as to how to make things better. They really want matters to improve, but they just haven't a clue about how to make that happen. For example, while arguing over how her boyfriend of two years seemed to show little interest in her, Yolanda threw in Jim's face the example of when he went out of his way early in their relationship to help his ex-girlfriend when she had a flat tire. Jim was angry that Yolanda brought up the past. While Yolanda probably should not have done that, her reasons for doing so had to do with the degree of her frustration with Jim. She had spoken to him before about how he had been showing less interest in her, and he didn't seem to be taking her seriously. So she said something she knew would aggravate him because she didn't know how else to get his attention.

DON'T OVERLOOK THE OBVIOUS

Physical or emotional exhaustion, health worries, financial woes, office politics, and simple hunger can prompt people to mistreat their loved ones. That kind of behavior may not be acceptable, but it is understandable. Give your mate a wide berth. If you ask "What's the matter?"

A good question to ask your mate is: Are you saying provocative things because you mostly want to hurt me or because there is something you don't think I understand yet?

and get a stinging reply, better to say, "It's obvious that something is on your mind. Take what time you need for yourself and maybe we can talk later. But please don't take it out on me. I've had a tense day, too."

REALIZE THAT YOUR MOOD AFFECTS YOUR JUDGMENT

You are not as objective as you think. If you're feeling unappreciated at work, you may have no tolerance when your mate "forgets" to pick up your dry cleaning. In contrast, if you are really happy that you succeeded at losing those extra twenty pounds, you might be very nurturing and sympathetic if your mate is in a grumpy mood. If you're feeling insecure about your partner's feelings toward you, then even his neutral actions (he tries to do fifty push-ups) may be taken personally ("he's trying to improve his appearance to attract someone else"). A good question to ask yourself is: If I was feeling really happy right now, would my mate's words or actions still bother me?

MEDITATE ON VIRTUES RATHER THAN VICES

Research shows that the most satisfied couples see virtues in their partners—virtues that their partners don't always see. An illusion? Wishful thinking? Probably to some extent but not completely. Think of these virtues: honesty,

patience, compassion, reliability, lovingness, generosity, optimism, perseverance, decisiveness, open-mindedness, tolerance, forgiveness, and kindness.
Which of these virtues does your partner more or less possess? Don't pretend
your mate is virtuous when you have obvious evidence against it, but don't
ignore the virtues he or she does possess. A good question to ask yourself is:
What qualities made me fall in love with this person in the first place? Am I
overlooking them?

When you make mistakes, when you say or do things you shouldn't, chances are
you cut yourself some slack and don't label yourself as bad, immoral, or mali-
cious. You look for reasons to justify your actions or to make your actions appear
less malevolent. Do the same for your partner.

3

why can't you be the one to change?

I t seemed like such a small thing. Betsy felt that she was overreacting, and yet something told her she had a right to be annoyed. Shouldn't her husband, Ned, call her when he knows he'll arrive home late? How many times had she worried that he was in an accident? How many times had she planned her schedule around his hours only to be forced to change her plans at the last minute? So she finally told Ned what she wanted. He agreed, but two days later he was almost thirty minutes late, and he never called. Betsy got angry, Ned got defensive. She told him he was inconsiderate. He said she was hard to please.

All Betsy wanted was for Ned to change in a small way. Was that too much to ask? Well . . .

∾ change is not a straight line

Some changes do come easily. You decide to switch careers and despite some anxiety you take the plunge. Or you ask your mate to be less critical or more tidy and lo and behold—he does it. But in most relationships, change is like molasses: slow, sticky, and a bit of a mess. Most couples believe that a reasonable request for change should be honored. They also believe that changes should come fairly quickly. But couples overlook many pitfalls to making and maintaining changes:

- There may be disagreement that changes are needed.
- There may be agreement that changes are needed but disagreement as to what those changes should be.
- Problems are defined in global rather than specific terms. Requesting that a partner "show respect" or "pay more attention" or "stop yelling" sounds reasonable. But those are subjective appraisals. A husband may believe he is paying more attention to his wife when he watches television with her, but she may regard that as insufficient. And the most common comeback to "Stop yelling!" is "I'm not yelling! I'm just raising my voice!"
- There may be agreement as to what changes are needed but disagreement on the strategies to make the changes.

How to Go About Making
Changes: Five Mind Traps to Avoid

Couples need to understand the process of change before it can take place. The most important changes will occur somewhat haphazardly, despite efforts to make them go smoothly.

It took Betsy and Ned about five months to work out their differences regarding the issue of his calling when running late. They fell into several traps along the way, which is why it took them so long.

MIND TRAP #1: CHANGE TAKES WILLPOWER

In relationships, it's a good idea to make sure that you aren't creating unnecessary problems for your mate who is trying to make changes. When Ned phoned Betsy to tell her he'd be late, she said thank you but was generally unenthusiastic. Ned later revealed that if she had given him a warm kiss when he arrived home or had told him once in a while that she appreciated his thoughtfulness, he might have not "forgotten" to call on other occasions. Betsy responded by saying that Ned "should" phone when he was going to be late. She did not think that gratitude was necessary on her part. So when Ned forgot to phone home, she concluded that he didn't have the willpower. But willpower without encouragement often fails.

MIND TRAP #2: A PARTNER HAS TO *WANT* TO CHANGE

Ned thought Betsy was being a tad unreasonable. He was often with customers when it was time to go home and he wasn't always able to interrupt them to make a phone call to Betsy and tell her he'd be late. On other days, traffic was particularly bad. He wished she'd understand that and cut him some slack. While Betsy knew that Ned was making sense, she felt that he was being too casual about how important the issue was to her. He always told her she was making a big deal out of nothing when she complained. She resented that attitude perhaps more than she resented his not calling. Betsy wanted him to *want* to call. Ned took offense, arguing that he should get credit for changing, especially if he didn't agree that the change was necessary.

Betsy could have helped her cause if she appreciated Ned's efforts instead of insisting that he agree with her position.

MIND TRAP #3: SETBACKS MEAN FAILURE

Slipups are inevitable. How you respond to a partner's backsliding is key. If you think your mate is trying to make changes, then it's best to ignore any slipups and respond with an uncritical curiosity. This is also a time to assess what precise goals you have. Ned thought that if he simply "improved," Betsy would be satisfied. But Betsy had a different goal in mind. She thought that if Ned forgot to call when he'd be late—even once—then he was being lax or inconsiderate. She wasn't satisfied with mere improvement. Once this difference in expectations was cleared up, Betsy decided that if Ned called "most of the time" when he was running late, she would be satisfied. Thus, Ned's "setback" was really an opportunity for them to review their situation and discover that they had misunderstood one another's expectations. Keep in mind that setbacks cannot occur unless there has already been progress.

MIND TRAP #4: CHANGES WILL COME EASIER OVER TIME

Ever start an exercise program and lose interest? Often, the hardest part of making changes is hanging in there after losing the initial motivation. It's important for each partner to focus on their progress and search for ways to continue to show encouragement and persistence. New behavioral changes must be anchored in place by repetition and reward, otherwise old patterns of behaving will have more weight and cause you to drift. Ned made the mistake of assuming that he could quickly create a new habit. But habits take time to form. Someone who is in the habit of calling a spouse each day to say hi will notice if an afternoon passes without making that phone call. But someone who hasn't formed that regular habit won't notice if days pass without calling. It's a good idea to monitor your progress *daily* for four to six weeks when making improvements in your relationship. Otherwise, you risk drifting back to the old ways of interacting.

MIND TRAP #5: THE CHANGES YOU REQUEST WILL MAKE YOU HAPPY

They might, but often they don't. That's because we sometimes misidentify what the real problem is. When we are dissatisfied in life—perhaps with ourselves or our jobs—we sometimes focus (wrongly) on our partner as the source of our dissatisfaction. Countless husbands and wives will tell a therapist, "I did change, but she still wasn't satisfied. I feel like nothing I do is ever good enough." Betsy wasn't as pleased as Ned thought she would be when he (finally) bought a cell phone so that he could call her from his car. Betsy later discovered that the phone situation was symbolic of a bigger issue: She felt taken for granted. She blamed Ned for that, but in reality she had felt taken for granted by her family (she also was the sibling who helped her brother and sisters when they needed help) and she felt unappreciated at work. Ironically, it took being dissatisfied with Ned's attempts to change before she realized that she had deeper concerns.

Tricky Business: Trying to Change a Chronic Problem

"Here we go again!" is a phrase many frustrated people utter in an otherwise loving relationship. It means that the same old argument is being recycled. The most common arguments are about time spent together (too much or too little), communication (too confusing), or sex (too tired). Just when a couple thinks they've hit upon a permanent solution, something happens to make the problem recur. If you've complained, pestered, sweet-talked, punished, or in any way tried to coerce your mate to change—and it hasn't worked—then your efforts have become part of the problem.

Trying to change a long-standing, repetitive problem requires a different approach than trying to change a recent problem. Long-standing problems have deeper roots and are usually made *more* resistant to change because of the tug-of-war in the relationship. When repeated efforts to get a partner to change have failed, the bad feelings that result (resentment over not being treated lovingly or fairly) complicate the situation. While common sense would tell you that the bad feelings would go away if the original problems were resolved, the truth is just the opposite: Until you can soften the hard feelings that have accumulated, you may not be able to resolve the underlying issues.

Long-standing problems bring another curious complication: Just when positive changes are happening, at least one partner will get angry, cynical, or fed up and thereby derail progress.

Liz and Karl fought regularly about money. He liked to control spending and would question Liz about every expense, no matter how minor. Understandably, Liz felt as if he was interrogating a witness and she resented it. Finally, they made an agreement whereby if a certain amount of money could be saved each week, Karl wouldn't question any of Liz's spending. Two weeks later Karl was pleased that their arguing had stopped and he told Liz that. Her response? "Yes, but look at all you put me through. Why couldn't you have been more understanding all along?" Her frustration was not unreasonable, but it had the effect of short-circuiting their progress by opening up an old wound. Remarks like Liz's (or similar remarks such as "It's about time!") are a sign that hurt feelings need to be soothed.

Before embarking on any effort to change a long-standing problem, partners need to say things that will make them feel closer and understood.

- "It must have been frustrating for you every time you asked me to make changes and all I did was argue back."
- "I was angry at you and not very cooperative. I'm sorry."
- "I resisted your efforts to get me to change because I didn't think you really understood my position. I should have tried to explain my position in a calm manner instead of being stubborn."
- "I guess neither of us took the time to really solve the problem. We just decided we were right and didn't want to compromise. I'm sorry for that."
- "When I ask myself what it must be like for you to have me around, I realize I'm not always the easiest person to live with."
- "I know we each made mistakes when we argued. I wish I hadn't said all those things that hurt you."
- "Thanks for putting up with me."

Those types of remarks should be repeated. Hurt feelings don't automatically heal overnight. By repeating those words once in a while, you are showing your mate that you take his or her feelings seriously and don't want to make the same mistakes again.

Often, if a couple approaches a chronic, unresolved problem with softer, more tender words, the solution to the problem falls more readily into place. Why? Because the sticking point in the argument is not your differing points of view (you say he's harsh with the kids; he says you're permissive, and so on). The usual sticking point is that one partner doesn't believe the other shows enough respect or caring. But softer words and a kinder approach show that a partner does care. Now, differing points of view can be examined more objectively.

HOW TO BREAK THE COMMUNICATION SOUND BARRIER

The most common problem for men is their difficulty opening up with their wives. When wives complain because conversational intimacy is lacking, men get "emotionally flooded" and shut down further. This leads to a vicious cycle where men won't open up for fear of causing an argument, which makes their wives angrier and more likely to argue. But when men do open up, their wives often criticize them.

HUSBAND (finally sharing personal thoughts): *Sometimes my job drives me crazy. I wish I had a different career, but I'd never make the same money I'm making now.*

WIFE (who has been begging him to open up): *Look, I have hard days, too. You don't see me complaining, do you?*

HUSBAND: *Why do I even bother talking to you?*

WIFE: *This is what a conversation is. What do you want me to do, say nothing?*

The wife's critical comments in the face of her husband's comments is akin to what happened to pilots who tried unsuccessfully to break the sound barrier. As they approached the speed of sound, their planes shook violently. Fearing the plane would break into pieces, the pilots veered off. (Pilot Chuck Yeager broke the sound barrier after he reasoned that the violent shaking would cease once the plane broke the speed of sound. He was right.) Untalkative husbands who finally try to open up are often responded to with criticism ("violent shaking") instead of enthusiasm from their long-frustrated wives. If men "veer off" as a way to avoid a "breakup," they never learn that if they'd only hang in there, the shaking would stop and a peaceful ride would be waiting for them on the other side of the barrier.

We like to think that making changes in a relationship is easy. It can be, but often it isn't. We improve our situation when we understand that changes take time and that setbacks will happen, and when we try to inject a kinder, more positive attitude into the conversations.

4
I'm right, you're wrong

Hanna wanted to fly across the country with her husband and child to attend a wedding. While she wasn't that close to the cousin who was to be married, most of her family would be there and she hadn't seen them in three years. She missed her parents and believed it was worth the cost to make the trip. Her husband, Dave, believed the trip was a waste of money.

"I don't care," Hanna said. "I want to see my family. You see your family whenever you want because they live nearby."

"I'm not saying you shouldn't see your family," Dave said. "All I'm saying is we don't have the money. Maybe we should wait."

"Yes, we do have the money."

"But we really can't afford it. It will wipe out our savings."

"Then why did you buy that expensive truck? You could have bought a perfectly good truck for five thousand dollars less and we would have had the money for the wedding. I told you that before, but you insisted you had to buy that particular truck."

"It has a high resale value," Dave said. "We'll save money in the long run."

Dave and Hanna often had conversations like this. The problem was that Dave basically wanted things to go his way, but he used logic as his cover. That way he denied his controlling style. He wasn't being dominant or dictatorial, he'd tell himself, just practical. Still, many people would rather be right and in control than truly happy in a give-and-take relationship. The early signs are there for each partner to recognize. It is a stupid mistake to ignore them.

The persistent need to be right in a relationship is a cancer. It may start out as small and insignificant, but it can eventually kill.

∾ you're not as smart as you think you are

Do these words sound familiar?

"It makes absolutely no sense to do it your way."
"No, you never said that. What you said was . . ."
"That never happened! How could you say such
     a thing?"
"That's a lie!"
"You don't know what you're talking about."
"If you look at all the facts, you'll see that my
     way makes sense."
"I know best."
"You're just being emotional. You're not looking
     at this logically."

Couples in relationships are truth-blind but they don't know it. Often, one person in the relationship (typically the male, but not always) believes his opinions and preferences are based on sound logic and reason. If his mate disagrees, she's wrong. Often, one person in the relationship (usually the female, but not always) believes that her memory is like a video camera and she knows only too well what her partner said or did on any given day. If her mate disagrees, he's wrong. Many people believe they know what their partner *meant* when he or she spoke, even if it wasn't actually *said*. When their partner disagrees, they are viewed as defensive, blind, or blatant liars.

Generally, partners in competition act that way for two reasons: It is a long-standing tendency based upon insecurity or arrogance in one or both individuals; or, it evolves over time as a response to a partner's controlling ways. The more your partner has to be right, the more you may challenge him. Eventually, he thinks *you* are the controlling and inflexible partner so he defends himself by taking as much control as he can. Cause and effect become interchangeable.

When one has to be right, the other must be wrong. For one to win, the other must lose. That's not teamwork. That's the work of adversaries.

Partners who must be right and get their way are not only controlling, they are *parental.* And the other partner becomes the child in that person's eyes. They always know better. They may think they have their partners' best interests at heart and may try (even sweetly) to persuade them of that, but basically they treat their mates as incapable, incompetent, or not quite up to the job.

Clues to the "I Know Better" Personality

A person who needs to be right often has opinions about many things. If your partner is a pediatrician, it makes sense that she might know best when it comes to medical ailments. But if she is an "I know better" spouse, she might also have strong views on how you dress, the right way to open wrapped presents, the best route to take on a trip, and the proper way for a salad to look. You are probably in a relationship with this type of controlling person when:

- You always have to explain and justify your actions (and usually your explanations are flawed).
- You debate insignificant issues.
- Your partner doesn't recognize personal preferences but sees only right and wrong.
- Your partner tells you that you are not the person she thought you were (unless you agree to do things her way).
- He tells you that you are trying to control him by getting your way, but when he wants his way it is because his way makes sense.
- You often feel disrespected even if she never actually calls you names or puts you down (your views are snickered at; she uses a condescending tone).
- He is allowed to make mistakes but you are not.
- She tends to ignore or interrupt you, or change the subject. Her opinions matter most.
- He shows anger but has a harder time showing genuine warmth or sadness or joy.

- If you get your way, your partner believes he "gave in" and that you should appreciate his "sacrifice."

This problem can be mild, moderate, or severe. In severe cases, it is really a form of verbal abuse. In milder cases, it reflects an insecure tendency by a person who simply feels more comfortable getting his way. Such people may also have careers where they do get their way, such as managers, police or military officers, doctors, or independent business owners.

Early Causes

One's background can play a part in the formation of this tendency. For example, men who grew up without a father (or whose father was physically present but psychologically absent or critical) *and* who had to take on extra responsibilities to help the family function, tend to fall into the "I know better" trap. Typically, these men grew up quickly and learned at an early age how to fend for themselves emotionally. They are very reliable workers and dedicated family men. They are anchors in troubled waters. But they are poor communicators (talking never got them much while growing up); and because they learned self-sufficiency early on, they don't like being told what to do. They often make important decisions without getting their partner's input. If they do ask for input, it is an afterthought, a polite gesture. They don't intend to change their mind. A subtle but powerful conflict for these men has to do with intimacy. They seek it because growing up they got less than they needed. But they flee from it because it means vulnerability. They don't want to depend too much on their partners. Consequently, being right is a way of preserving their identity in a context of emotional closeness that otherwise would seem too threatening.

Children raised by perfectionistic (and, therefore, often disapproving) parents may also grow into adults who need to be right. In effect, they are still trying to prove themselves as worthy. To be disagreed with is to be told they are not only wrong, but also unworthy. Thus, to feel worthy they must be right. Some people rebel against such a background and try to be flexible, open-minded, easygoing people. However, they may end up marrying someone who needs to be right.

While people who need to be right often deal with facts and figures and cold logic to express their version of the truth, some people use their emotions.

When Steve told Laura he didn't like the feel of the new bedsheets she'd bought, she told him he hurt her feelings.

"But I didn't mean to," he said. "I just don't like these sheets. They make my legs itch."

"It doesn't matter what you think," Laura said. "The fact is you hurt my feelings. My feelings are not right or wrong, they just are."

Now Steve was in a bind. If he apologized, he'd feel annoyed because he really didn't think he said anything wrong. But if he told her she was overreacting, he knew she'd be angry.

While the masculine version of "I'm right" uses facts as weapons to get leverage, the feminine version uses feelings. If one person "knows" that investing in a computer makes more sense than investing in a vacation, you can't argue with him. If another person says that her feelings are her feelings, how does one argue with that? It is a standoff. The real truth is that feelings can be distorted just as easily as facts. And even if the facts are clear, and the feelings are indisputable, so what?

> *Relationships are built on mutual give-and-take, not the ability to successfully build your case like a prosecuting attorney.*

How to Stop Needing to Be Right

Changing this pattern takes time and patience.

REALIZE THAT BEING RIGHT ISN'T WHAT'S IMPORTANT

If you insist that being right is most important, your relationship will suffer. In fact, it will probably fail. Being fair and generous is more likely to help your relationship succeed. Don't believe your own propaganda—that the real issue is the facts and logic of your viewpoint. The real issue is whether you will abandon your need to be dominant in favor of a relationship that runs on fairness and mutual goodwill.

STAY FLEXIBLE

Research shows that very satisfied couples use a rule of thumb whereby some disagreements are resolved by allowing one partner more decision-making power when the issue at hand is more important to that partner. So, if you love to garden, maybe you should have more say in determining which equipment to purchase. If your mate is a music aficionado, maybe he should have final say over what stereo speakers to buy. The problem is that people with a strong need to be right often convince themselves that the topic is important to them and therefore they claim the right to make the final decision. Monitor how often your need to be right shows itself. Then decide that being friends is more important than being right.

CONSIDER BOTH PARTNERS' DESIRES

In the opening of this chapter, Hanna wanted to fly cross-country for a family reunion. Dave insisted it was too costly, even though he had recently purchased an expensive truck. A solution that would meet both needs would be to discuss ways of cutting back other expenses so that the trip could be made and the bank account wouldn't be wiped out. Had Dave been more aware of his need to get his way months earlier, he might have purchased a less expensive truck while using the difference to pay for the trip.

PRAISE COLLABORATION AND NEGOTIATION

Show your partner that you appreciate his efforts to be accommodating. It isn't easy for him to back off when he believes he's right.

BE AWARE OF EMOTIONAL WITHDRAWAL

Remember, a person with a strong need to be right is trying to preserve a sense of self that she feels is threatened if she must "give in." So she may react to compromises by pulling away emotionally. Agree ahead of time that you will discuss this situation when it occurs. She needs to learn that getting closer is not threatening. It takes time and a willingness to take emotional risks.

If you need to be right all the time, you're wrong.

If all else fails, agree to flip a coin every time there is a disagreement that cannot be resolved satisfactorily. Whoever wins gets his or her way. The benefit of this is that it ensures fairness and cuts down on useless (and endless) debates. Also, this strategy eventually motivates a couple to resolve matters without having to resort to a coin toss.

5

it's just a fantasy. or is it?

Tim and Wendy attended their friend's thirtieth birthday party. At one point, Wendy overheard Tim and his friends discussing various female celebrities whom they thought were very sexy. It was obvious from their conversation that many of the men had fantasized about having sex with these women.

The conversation did not surprise Wendy. What surprised her was Tim's admission that he fantasized about other women much more often than she realized. On the drive home, Wendy was upset and asked Tim for more details. He admitted having fantasies but downplayed the issue.

"I may *think* about other women," he said. "But I *stay* with you."

Wendy wasn't satisfied. "Oh, and I suppose you want me to believe that you never fantasize about these women when we're making love?"

"Sometimes, but not often. It's not a big deal."

"Not a big deal?" Wendy said, raising her voice. "I think it means you are not satisfied with me and that you'd rather be with someone else!"

Wendy's concern was not unusual. In fact, 25 to 30 percent of people either feel guilty about sexual fantasies or believe they are a sign of relationship problems. What is myth and what is reality?

Sexual concerns can sometimes lead to sexual disorders. Misinformation is a common cause of sexual difficulties. While some disorders need to be treated medically or psychologically, it is common for sexual "disorders" to vanish when people are educated about sexual myths.

Sexual disorders fall into four categories:

1. *Desire.* Typically, low sexual desire is a cause of concern for many people, particularly as they age. Sexual addiction, however, is a form of intense, compulsive desire. Mismatched desire—when spouses are frequently not in sync with each other, or if one spouse is routinely dissatisfied with the frequency of sex—is not a disorder but can be a problem for some couples.
2. *Arousal.* Inability for a man to get or keep an erection, or inability for a woman to become adequately lubricated.
3. *Orgasm.* Inability to achieve orgasm, or to have delayed orgasms.
4. *Pain during intercourse.* This can occur at any age for a woman but often happens after menopause when vaginal tissue is thinner and drier.

Believing any of the common sexual myths can cause or worsen sexual disorders.

꩜ strip your mind of seven sexual myths

Was Wendy right or wrong? Would it be better for Tim to have few, if any, sexual fantasies? Does loyalty to one's partner require not having fantasies about others?

Myth #1: Sexual Fantasies Signify Relationship Problems

Studies show that 95 percent of the adult population have daily sexual fantasies. Men are likely to have twice as many fantasies as women, but women's fantasies are no less intense. (Romance novels are read almost exclusively by women. These books contain highly erotic passages.) Furthermore, sexual fantasies are associated with increased satisfaction in one's sex life. The more sexually active a person is, the more likely he or she will be to sexually fantasize.

Still, a substantial minority of people believe sexual fantasies are wrong, particularly fantasies about people other than one's mate. They believe it is a form of cheating and feel dishonest about not revealing their fantasies (only about 25 percent of people disclose them to their partner). Interestingly, most of these people are young.

But what about fantasizing about other lovers, especially while making love to one's partner? First of all, sexual fantasies about others are common. However, the most common fantasy is about one's mate. Not surprisingly, such fantasies occur mostly when one is *not* having sex with his or her partner. While making love, sexual fantasies are more likely to be about what will happen next in the current sexual encounter, which is more about anticipation than fantasy.

Not all sexual fantasizing is harmless. If your marriage is unsatisfying, regular fantasies about others— especially about someone whom you are attracted to and whom you know—will pull you further away from your mate. You may be less inclined to resolve any relationship problems because you fantasize about being with someone else.

> *As people become more mature sexually, they are less likely to see any harm in sexual fantasies. This is probably due to the fact that more sexual experience is associated with involvement in a committed relationship where trust is higher.*

Compulsive sexual fantasizing or fantasies that lead a person to treat others as sex objects (one-night stands, seeking prostitutes, etc.) are degrading and ignore the full dimensions of what makes us human. But all else being equal, sexual fantasies are not a sign of relationship problems and are usually a sign of sexual interest and satisfaction.

Myth #2: Being Concerned About One's Own Sexual Gratification Is Selfish

Taken to an extreme, this is absolutely true. There is no question that giving enjoyment to your partner is very important for a relationship. But in order to receive properly, your mate must be willing to abandon his or her preoccupation with you and focus exclusively on his or her own enjoyment. This is not selfishness, this is a requirement. If your mate is trying to please you, shouldn't you accept the gift fully? The key is give-and-take. Taking turns allows each of you to focus on giving and receiving—and not always at the same time. Simultaneous give-and-take is fine. But don't limit yourself to mutual responding. Sometimes, give more than you receive. At other times, take more than you give. It's not only okay, it will make for a more exhilarating experience.

Myth #3: Sex Must Always Be Great

If you believe this, you will be disappointed more often than you need to be. Sex can't always be terrific, but it can still be satisfying. Fatigue, hassles with the kids, insufficient time, aches and pains, relationship strains, medical problems, mild depression, and a host of other factors can make the experience more mechanical and less exciting. Still, the opportunity to be closer with your mate may be worth it, even if the fireworks fizzle. The more anxious you are about performance or the newer your relationship, the more you might fear that unless sex is dynamic, it's a dud.

There are two common mistakes that add to the myth that sex must always be great. The notion that a man must maintain his erection the entire time, otherwise it means he is not that interested, is simply not true. The state of arousal can vary during sex, especially if partners are enjoying a long lovemaking session and taking time for pleasures that are not always genitally focused. Men may feel uneasy about losing all or part of their erection during foreplay, but they fail to realize that women's arousal varies, too. It is just easier to notice on a man. When a couple is truly at ease with one another, a temporary reduction in arousal is not considered a problem.

The other common mistake is believing that reaching orgasm is vital for sexual satisfaction. If that were so, women would be sexually satisfied about 60 percent of the time. That's how often, on average, they reach orgasm. (The rate is highest among married women. About 75 percent of married women say they usually or always have orgasms.) Many men and women believe they are doing something wrong if a woman can't climax every time. It simply isn't true. In fact, many couples discover that sex without orgasm once in a while (men, this is for you, too) improves the quality of their foreplay. It can also be tantalizing (or relaxing) to work your partner up to near-orgasm but then stop short. There is no strong correlation between sexual satisfaction and frequency of orgasm.

The best aphrodisiac is not fantasy, experimentation, or the influence of drugs or alcohol. The research is unequivocal that most sexual satisfaction occurs in the context of a loving, committed relationship. Satisfaction and enjoyment of sex has more to do with a high level of marital/relationship adjustment than it has to do with age or any other factor.

Myth #4: Sex Makes Everything All Right

Wouldn't it be great if that were so? Solving problems and improving the relationship quality would be a simple physical exercise. Usually, having sex means that things can't be all that bad. It reassures us. But it doesn't fix the problems. Men are more prone to believe that sex fixes everything, which is one reason many women pull back from sex when problems have gotten worse. They don't want to give the man the idea that everything is fine. Men are better at denying or minimizing relationship problems. Often, matters have to get completely out of hand before many men stand up and take notice. Needing reassurance that the problems are fixable, these men seek sex. But when they get sex, they unfortunately convince themselves that their women are feeling better and that the problems are fading into the background.

Sex can help warm up a relationship that needs warming, and it can be pure joy when love is mutual, deep, and devoted. But it does not make everything all right.

Myth #5: Engaging in Sex Halfheartedly Has Negative Results

This tends to be true if you do this out of fear of causing problems should you resist—which is also a clue that your relationship is unhealthy and that you may not be emotionally mature enough for a sexual relationship. Also, a partner who often pressures you into having sex when you are not interested is probably being selfish.

Still, in a recent study of young women age thirty or younger, the three most common reasons for engaging in sex halfheartedly were a desire to please their partner, to promote intimacy, and to avoid relationship tension. Most couples who are secure in their relationship will admit having said yes to sex when they would rather have said no. Often, such spontaneous excursions end up being pleasant, if not downright fun. "Quickies," especially at a time when having sex is not at the top of your list, can be invigorating and playful.

Myth #6: Low Sexual Desire Always Means Something Is Wrong

It can mean something is wrong. Depression, for instance, or chronic fatigue, or certain medical conditions can weaken one's sexual drive. So can dissatisfaction with one's physical appearance. Low desire might indicate a relationship problem, but it depends on whether it is a chronic or occasional condition.

What is considered normal when it comes to sexual desire? In a classic study reported in the *New England Journal of Medicine,* one hundred educated and married couples, with an average age of thirty-three, were examined. All of these couples reported that their marriages were happy and satisfying. Still, half the men and 77 percent of the women reported an occasional lack of interest in sex. One-third had sex less than once a week. Ten percent had sex less than once a month. (It is worth noting that 40 percent of the men reported occasional erectile or ejaculatory problems, and 63 percent of the women reported occasional problems with arousal or orgasm. Sexual perfection is not the norm for most happy couples.)

If you say yes to sex (when you'd rather say no), make sure that your partner is devoted to you, not just devoted to having sex with you.

If low sexual desire persists and you don't know why, see your doctor. But don't automatically believe it is abnormal to lose your interest once in a while or not be continually focused on sex.

Myth #7: Sexual Experimentation Is Aberrant Behavior

It depends on what you mean by experimentation. Sex with children, animals, or inanimate objects are disorders. Masochism and sadism are also considered illnesses.

Most sexual experimentation by couples takes the form of discovering new positions, or making love outdoors, using body oils, going to a hotel or getaway, showering together or swimming in the nude, or wearing sexy underwear. In a major survey, half of all couples said they experimented sexually once in a while. They were twice as likely to report sexual satisfaction than couples who did not experiment. The study also revealed that sexual experimentation was a far better predictor of overall sexual satisfaction than frequency of lovemaking.

Experimentation can be misapplied, however. Partners may be pressured to engage in sexual acts that they view as immoral or distasteful. While some experimentation can loosen up rigid beliefs, not all preferences are irrational. For example, about 25 percent of the population have engaged in anal intercourse at some point during their lifetime (and 10 percent tried it in the past year). That is a significant number, but it also means that 75 percent of couples never try it. Many coercive partners use pornography to show their partners various sexual practices. Then they claim that those practices are obviously common and normal. But that may be far from the truth. Some people certainly are sexually prudish. But if you enjoy sex, and you know you have engaged in most of the common variations of sex, then chances are good that any discomfort you have about some sexual activity should be respected. If in doubt, talk to trusted friends or experts. Don't believe the propaganda that if you really loved your partner you'd do anything that he or she wants sexually. Sexual freedom means the freedom to say no.

6

we know what
we're arguing about

Rob and Kate were grocery shopping. While Kate was comparing prices of shampoo, Rob lingered in the greeting card section.

"Who did you buy a card for?" Kate asked.

"Heather," Rob said. Then he hastened to add, "It's her birthday next week."

Heather was Rob's old girlfriend. He broke up with her about a year before he met Kate. Heather was recently married and lived a thousand miles away. Kate tossed a bottle of shampoo into her cart and stared at Rob. "Didn't you just send her a card?"

"That was for Christmas," Rob said. He detected Kate's dissatisfaction. "Look, I'm happy that she's married and I thought she might like a card with a note on how I'm doing. That's all. Why are you so jealous?"

"Did I say I was jealous? I just don't understand why you have to go out of your way to buy her another card when she's married and you haven't even seen her in three years. I think you still carry a torch for her."

"I'm not carrying a torch. And I'm buying the card," he said defiantly. "It's a perfectly innocent thing to do."

They finished their grocery shopping without saying another word. Later at home Kate brought up the subject again. She told Rob there must be more to his interest in Heather. He vehemently denied it. Then he told Kate he would continue to mail Heather letters whenever he felt like it.

What was going on? In her heart, Kate knew that Heather was not a threat. What really bothered her? And Rob believed that writing to Heather was not all that important to him, yet he was insistent.

Kate and Rob were making an all too common mistake. They believed that their argument was really about the topic at hand. As a result, it would be an argument that would resurface and never get resolved, because they weren't really arguing about Heather at all. So what were they arguing about? We'll get to that later in the chapter.

ℵ uncover hidden agendas

A hidden agenda is an unspoken, sometimes subconscious issue that fuels upset feelings. When couples argue repeatedly and old conflicts show up again and again, you can bet that a hidden agenda is lurking. Until it surfaces and is resolved, conflicts or resentments will persist.

Here are some clues that hidden agendas are operating:

- The same argument repeats itself, even when you thought it was fixed.
- Just when one argument is settled, another issue soon erupts.
- Conflicts are marked by inflammatory or attacking language. Name-calling, or use of words that are exaggerated or dramatic such as "Grow up!" or "You always . . ." or "You never . . ." indicate intense feelings that have carried over from some other unresolved issue.
- Anger over "little things."
- Solutions and/or agreements that never get acted on or that quickly get forgotten.
- Frequent irritability with your mate.
- Passive-aggressive behavior such as snubbing a partner, sulking, "forgetting" something that was important to your mate, running late, taking your time when your mate is in a rush, etc.

Sometimes you may be well aware of your hidden agendas. But you may choose not to bring them up because you fear it will cause more problems or will hurt your partner's feelings.

When couples argue but do not identify hidden agendas that may be lurking, all their efforts to problem-solve or communicate effectively will be a bandage at best and probably useless. Whatever understanding they reach or solution they agree to will be ineffective because the deeper problem is being overlooked. It's like giving aspirin for a fever but ignoring the underlying infection that caused the fever.

> *Claiming "We can't communicate" is sometimes a misrepresentation. Many couples could communicate more effectively if they were discussing what really mattered.*

When hidden agendas remain, communication will likely break down and one or both will regard the other as stubborn or refusing to listen. What they may not appreciate is that communication *must* break down because what needs to be discussed is being dismissed. The discussion must, inevitably, go nowhere.

Ignored, hidden agendas are like an infection. Bad feelings develop and become cumbersome to sort through. These bad feelings cause more arguments as partners grow crankier with each other and become less interested in going out of their way for one another.

Types of Hidden Agendas

Esteemed researcher Dr. John Gottman at the University of Washington has had a huge impact on our understanding of how couples relate. He introduced the concept of hidden agendas. While it might seem that hidden agendas could be quite numerous, there are fundamentally only three categories:

1. *Am I cared about? Loved?* If you secretly question this, you may find yourself arguing or fretting over many issues. If you find yourself thinking, "If he loved me or cared about me he would . . . ," then this agenda may be operating.
2. *Is my partner responsive? Interested in me? Does he show his love?* You may believe that your mate loves you, but you may still be hungry for evidence. If this agenda is operating, you will make demands of your partner or be dissatisfied with any token signs of affection.
3. *Is this relationship fair?* If not, you will feel in a one-down position. You may then try to get control in some way so as to balance the scales.

In the opening of the chapter we met Rob and Kate. They argued over the fact that Rob was writing cards to his former girlfriend. Their arguments got nowhere until the hidden agendas were uncovered. Kate was the first to try to mend fences.

"Rob," she said. "I probably shouldn't have been so hardheaded this afternoon. Your writing to Heather is really not a big deal to me. I know she isn't a threat to our relationship."

"Then why did you practically accuse me of lusting after her?"

"I was angry, but I couldn't figure out the real reason. But after thinking it through, I now understand what bothered me. It was the fact that you wanted to take the time to write to her—even tell her about your life—when I've been feeling neglected by you for quite some time. You don't talk much, you never were much of a talker. That bothers me sometimes, but it bothers me more when you write to her instead. I wish you'd send me a card once in a while."

Kate was being open and vulnerable. Rob got defensive at first and even told her she was being silly. Actually, he was relieved that the problem was being resolved, but he made the mistake of minimizing Kate's feelings. She didn't think her concerns were silly. Fortunately, Kate didn't jump down his throat and Rob opened up, too.

"I don't know why I was so insistent that I would keep writing to Heather. She really doesn't mean anything to me. I guess I've been feeling kind of pushed around lately. Especially at work, but sometimes by you. Remember how I told you I didn't want to go grocery shopping today, but you insisted I go with you."

Now it was Kate's turn to be a bit defensive. "I said that because I knew we'd be sure to get everything we wanted if both of us went. Whenever one of us goes alone we forget things."

"Yes, but I told you earlier I was tired and you paid no attention. So I came along to avoid an argument, but I really resented it."

"So you'd like me to think about ways I might be taking charge unfairly, is that right?" Kate asked.

"Yes. And I guess you'd like me to talk more to you."

Kate and Rob handled this conversation very well. It became obvious that each had a hidden agenda. Kate's had to do with responsiveness and Rob's with fairness. By discussing their concerns openly, they were able to come up with a plan that might fix these problems in the future. At least it was a good start. And it had nothing to do with Heather at all.

Couples argue or disagree about many potential topics. Sometimes the topics they discuss are really the issue. But as you saw with Rob and Kate, the topics being discussed may be the tip of the iceberg. Underneath are the more substantial concerns. Examine the repetitive arguments below and the agendas that might underlie them:

REPETITIVE ARGUMENT: *I want to go to my parents' house this weekend.*
POSSIBLE HIDDEN AGENDA: *If you loved me you'd go.*

REPETITIVE ARGUMENT: *You spent how much?*
POSSIBLE HIDDEN AGENDA: *You're not being fair.*

REPETITIVE ARGUMENT: *You're too lenient (harsh) with the kids!*
POSSIBLE HIDDEN AGENDA: *You're too harsh with me.*

REPETITIVE ARGUMENT: *Stop interrupting when I talk!*
POSSIBLE HIDDEN AGENDA: *You're not showing me respect or love.*

REPETITIVE ARGUMENT: *Why were you late again?*
POSSIBLE HIDDEN AGENDA: *You're not interested in me.*

REPETITIVE ARGUMENT: *Stop pawing at me!*
POSSIBLE HIDDEN AGENDA: *You don't care about me, only yourself.*

REPETITIVE ARGUMENT: *Why don't you ever show me any affection?*
POSSIBLE HIDDEN AGENDA: *You're not responsive to my needs.*

REPETITIVE ARGUMENT: *I always do what you want. Why won't you do what I want for a change?*
POSSIBLE HIDDEN AGENDA: *This relationship isn't fair.*

If you think a hidden agenda exists, you must dig for it and then discuss it. Be aware of the frustrations that accumulate when you mistake what the argument was really about.

What to Say and How to Say It

When you think that a problem is being fueled by a hidden agenda, first stop the discussion and bring up the underlying issue.

SAY: *I just realized something. What we are arguing about is really just a symbol for an underlying concern I have. Let me explain my concern as best as I can.*

OR SAY: *You keep getting upset with me about this. Is it possible that something else is bothering you? Do you worry that I don't care about you or that the relationship is unfair?*

DON'T SAY: *You know what's really got me so damn angry? I'll tell you. I can't believe I just figured it out, but it makes so much sense. I'm angry because you really don't give a crap about me . . .*

When you've stated your underlying concern, add phrases of support or empathy for your partner so he will be able to listen to you with less defensiveness.

SAY: *No wonder you've been frustrated with our conversations. I'd keep getting upset about little things like the messy floor or how much time you spend on the computer, but I was really worried that you'd lost interest in me. I'm glad I figured it out, aren't you?*

OR SAY: *You must have felt very aggravated at times, especially when all we did was argue. But I'm glad I figured out what was really bothering me and I'm hoping you can listen patiently to my concerns.*

DON'T SAY: *Now that I've figured out what's really bothering me, are you going to listen or be as uncooperative as always?*

Hidden agendas are like weeds. They crop up everywhere, even in beautiful gardens and satisfying relationships. But they need to be dug out if you want to prevent unnecessary arguments or a deepening dissatisfaction.

When the underlying agendas of caring, responsiveness, or fairness have been explained by each of you, don't continue the same old fight or bring up more examples that will inflame the situation. Instead, focus on solutions—what you need your partner to do so that your underlying fears can eventually be put to rest. Make your ideas specific.

SAY: *I guess I feel that I do most of the work around here including the child care. I know you help out, but I don't think it's been as fair as I need it to be. Could we discuss ways you can help out more? I'm interested in your thoughts.*

OR SAY: *I know you love me, but I've been feeling neglected lately. Maybe you have, too. I'd like to come up with some specific ways to fix this. Some of my ideas include giving each other a back massage each night, going out to a movie at least once a month, and maybe planning a weekend getaway. What do you think?*

DON'T SAY: *You'd better start paying more attention to me! I'm only your wife, after all. You pay more attention to your truck than you do to me.*

Finally, it's important to touch base with your partner about your progress. Don't presume that your mate is feeling better because you know you've been trying hard. He or she might not be noticing all of your efforts. If you have made progress, tell your mate thanks. It needs to be said and just as important, it needs to be heard.

7

the kids will get over it

I hear these questions every week from people who call my office.

If I get a divorce, will my kids be okay eventually?

How can I emotionally protect my children during the separation?

What's the best way to minimize pain and problems for my children after the divorce?

Is it best to end a marriage when I'm not happy, or remain in it for the sake of my kids but be miserable?

Getting remarried will probably help my children, at least economically, right?

This chapter will answer those questions and many others. The answers are not for the faint of heart. Separation and divorce is a very complicated process. When studying the effects, we must take into consideration dozens of variables such as the child's age at separation, amount of conflict in the home, parental mental health, parenting skills, gender and temperament of the child, whether or not a re-marriage has occurred, and so on. There are literally thousands of research studies, and many findings are contradictory. Still, a consensus has emerged. Experts can reasonably predict the typical consequences of separation and divorce on children, though obviously some kids will fare much better than others.

Drawing conclusions about research is also complicated in part because researchers and other experts often have their own agendas. Extremists on both sides of the issue have fogged up the picture. For example, many people believe that a couple should never divorce. They view staying married as always preferable. But the truth is that some children are better off when their parents divorce. Others want to dismiss findings that show negative effects of divorce on children. They are concerned that it might turn back the clock to days when commitment was paramount and people remained in miserable marriages. They view permanent commitment as a pipe dream and less important than an individual's freedom of choice to carry on with any relationship that satisfies them. Anything that restricts choice is bad. It is true, however, that the upsurge in divorce has had negative, long-lasting effects on our children and our culture.

If you are already divorced, you will want to read this chapter and find out how to best help your children. If you are contemplating a separation or divorce, this chapter will hopefully encourage you to do all you can to improve your marriage enough so that you will want to remain married. If you are happily married, this chapter will motivate you to stay that way.

◌ your children are vulnerable

There is a common psychological tendency that occurs when we act in ways that run counter to our attitudes or standards. Imagine a person who regards herself as kind and compassionate but then one day acts unkindly. How will she handle that contradiction? She might change her view about herself and conclude that she is not a very kind person after all. But most likely she will keep her view of herself by coming up with excuses for her behavior. *I shouldn't have been unkind, but he deserved it!* she might think. Or else she'll pretend that her actions weren't unkind after all. She'll distort what her conscience is telling her is true in order to maintain her positive view of herself.

This is a common tendency among parents who separate or divorce. They've heard the reports that show how children suffer when parents split up. But since they need to maintain their view of themselves as good parents who would not purposely do anything that would hurt their children, they now must convince themselves that the suffering will ultimately be in their children's best interest (*My kids would be worse off if I stayed married.*) or they must minimize the negative effects of divorce (*Their hurt will be temporary, then they'll adjust.*). While this distortion helps the parents feel better, it poses a danger to their children. It is a mistake parents must try to avoid.

> *If parents deny or minimize the negative effects of divorce, they will not take all the necessary steps to truly help their children.*

Another outcome is possible, too. In order to minimize guilt feelings, a parent might unfairly demonize his or her partner as a way to justify the divorce. But such a demonization will cause parental conflict and more important, may adversely affect a child's relationship with that other parent and with the child's self-esteem.

I have watched family and friends divorce. Most couples deeply love their children, so their decision to divorce did not come without considerable anxiety and pain. I don't want parents to feel worse than they already do. But I don't want them to pretend or ignore the dangers. Parents do the right thing when they view separation or divorce as something that can potentially cause some damage to their children—damage that may even affect their children's adult lives—and use their pain of regret as motivation to do what it takes to not add to the damage.

Why Do Kids Suffer?

Most parents who divorced in the 1990s had children under six years of age. About 40 percent of white children and 75 percent of African-American children will experience a divorce by the time they reach sixteen. Nearly 40 percent of children will experience a *second* parental divorce by age eighteen.

The idea that divorce is a one-time event that children will soon adjust to is outdated. Divorce is a process with many transitions that occur over years.

- First there is the marital conflict, which can be intense and open, or milder and behind closed doors.
- Then there is the separation. Kids must adapt to seeing one parent at a time.
- Typically, behavior problems emerge, especially in boys; and depression occurs, especially in girls. Academic scores often decline. But even if grades don't drop, problems may exist. Some kids cope with loss by wanting to be

perfect. They may blame themselves for the divorce (kids under age ten are most likely to do this) and fear doing anything else that will upset a parent or bring on parental rejection.

- Usually, the strain of separation takes a toll on parents who then become less effective. "Diminished parenting" is a term used to describe this phenomenon. Here, parents become inconsistent disciplinarians. Consistency requires planning, monitoring, and patience—something that single parents have in short supply. Parents often expect more mature behavior from their kids after a separation. Kids are expected to help out more and fend for themselves. Parental supervision is typically less than it would be if parents were still together, and many older kids are more at risk for drinking, drug use, or promiscuous behavior due to looser parental oversight.

- Kids must hang in there while parents hammer out a separation agreement, a process that can lead to much arguing and tension between parents. Many children find themselves in the middle, especially when parental disagreements over finances result in character assaults that the children overhear. (When each parent blames the other for the breakup or for the inability to settle the legal agreements in a cooperative manner, who is likely to accept the blame? The kids. Most kids feel responsible for the parental breakup despite efforts by their parents to dissuade them of that notion.)

- Then the children must eventually cope with their parents' new partners. There may be many such partners and more breakups. The divorce rate for *remarried* women under age forty is 62 percent. That rate climbs much higher if the woman already has children.

- If a parent remarries, a child must adapt to this new lifestyle that may include stepsiblings or half-siblings, a new home, and possibly a new school.

- The process continues. It is sad but true that most divorced fathers see their children five times a year or less. It may start out with frequent visits, but as the children age and want more time with friends, parent time is compromised. More often, one parent relocates far enough away to make regular visitation impossible. Noncustodial fathers who remarry tend to spend less time with their children. That time drops even more if the father has children with his new partner and devotes more energy to his new family.

It is unwise for any parent to automatically believe that their children will cope well and that a divorce is a brief crisis. Some children may cope better than other children, and they may handle some aspects of the divorce better than other aspects, but they will inevitably struggle. Some have adjustment problems for several years. Most children improve over time (rarely do they have no scars) but may still suffer somewhat. By some estimates, about one-third of the children of divorced parents will get worse or still be floundering years after the divorce.

FREQUENTLY ASKED QUESTIONS

Is divorce ever beneficial for my children? Yes. The best evidence reveals that children in *high-conflict* homes (much yelling, verbal or physical abuse) where the parents remain married show *worse* adjustment (more severe and more persistent behavior and academic problems) than do children from divorced families. However, while divorce helps children from high-conflict homes, they are still worse off than children from intact, low-conflict homes. The best solution for kids from high-conflict homes is for their parents to work things out and reduce conflict. But that solution requires intense dedication on the part of the parents.

Does divorce affect boys differently than girls? The findings are inconsistent, but on average boys are more likely to "act out" (aggression, behavior problems) and girls are more likely to "act in" (depression, worry, isolation). Some studies indicate that divorced mothers have more conflicts with sons than daughters and are likely to be more punitive. That may be due to the fact that the boys are in fact more aggressive and provoke more anger on the part of their mothers.

Is it accurate to say that kids generally cope better over time? Yes, but new research findings challenge that statement. Typically, kids can adapt over time and show fewer disturbances—usually over the course of a few years. But that happens only if there is regular involvement by both parents and if the parents' post-divorce relationship is harmonious. That's a tall order. Furthermore, new studies suggest that the evidence for improvement over time was misleading because researchers tended to focus on the immediate months and years following a divorce, not what happens into adulthood.

What is the effect of divorce on children as they enter adulthood? New findings suggest that some of the negative effects of divorce won't show up until the child is dating, having sexual relations, or married. These children grow up to be adults who are more wary of marriage, less trusting, and less able to resolve interpersonal conflicts than peers from intact families. Men and women from divorced homes tend to view their marital role as less important than do adults from intact homes. In a study using a representative sample of American youth, children whose parents had divorced before the kids were sixteen were evaluated when they were between eighteen and twenty-two years of age. Sixty-five percent had poor relationships with their fathers, and 30 percent had poor relationships with their mothers. Twenty-five percent had dropped out of high school, and 40 percent had sought psychological counseling. These figures were twice as high as those of young adults from intact families. The young adults whose parents had divorced when they were age six or younger had slightly higher chances of dropping out of high school and were more likely to seek psychological counseling than children who were older when their parents divorced.

Are there any other long-term effects of divorce? A 1997 study compared mortality of divorced from non-divorced children. Basically, divorced children can expect to live an average of four fewer years. The divorced child's previous health status, temperament, or socioeconomic status could not explain this difference. Children of divorce are more likely to divorce, to smoke, and to receive less of an education—all of which can reduce one's life expectancy. Interestingly, a comparison group of children who had lost a parent due to death had the same life expectancy as children whose parents remained alive. So it is not parental loss *per se* that lowers mortality in children of divorce. There is something more.

Do children fare better when a parent dies than when parents divorce? Surprisingly, that is true. Studies show that children do have conduct and academic problems after a parent dies, but only to half the extent that children of divorce do. These children are also more likely to hold a more positive view of marriage and commitment than children of divorce.

Is the overall effect of divorce devastating? Some studies show dramatic negative effects on personality, academics, and behavioral or emotional disturbance. However, the majority of studies show negative effects that are modest, even trivial. Again, it all depends on many other factors. Divorce is not a simple life transition that a child handles like a Little League team handles a setback. Divorcing parents prefer to imagine that children are resilient and that life's hardships can be managed effectively given time and support. But such a view is often wishful thinking and ignores child development. Children are impressionable. Early life experiences have profound effects on a person's outlook and coping style. Harder to measure are the subjective effects that may not hamper one's life but still hurt. Young adults who came from high-conflict homes often say that the divorce was a relief. But most kids from divorced homes where conflict was low or moderate wished their parents had stayed together. As adults, they look upon the divorce as something sad and painful, and their own divorce rates are higher.

Doesn't remarriage benefit children? Isn't it better to have two adults in a home instead of just one? These findings may surprise you. On average, the only benefit of remarriage to children is financial. Kids in a remarriage are no better off than kids living with just one custodial parent when it comes to psychological adjustment. Remarriage is not the automatic balm that will soothe or heal broken hearts. In fact, the reverse is sometimes true. Stepfamily situations, while potentially wonderful and beneficial, often create more problems. Remarried parents are usually less satisfied with their new partner's parenting skills than they were with their former spouse's skills. Stepparent relations with a child are more strained. Loyalty conflicts may emerge. Many stepfamilies are loving and healthy. Most stepparents should be praised because they have a difficult job. Still, remarriages end in divorce more often than first marriages, especially when children are part of the picture.

So, What's a Loving, Devoted Parent to Do?

The situation isn't hopeless. The negative effects of divorce can be reduced, though not eliminated, if parents pay attention to key Do's and Don'ts. These are not easy to accomplish, but they are necessary.

DO'S

Allow your ex as much time with the children as possible. Regular involvement is essential, frequent involvement is better. The less time a child spends with one parent, the worse it is. If a father's involvement with the child was low prior to the separation, it will probably stay low. However, increasing that involvement can improve father-child relations. Obviously, if your ex was abusive or neglectful, this rule does not apply. But be careful. Don't let animosity toward your ex cause you to exaggerate his or her faults. If your ex is a decent parent, he or she deserves as much of a relationship as possible with your child.

Encourage and enhance your former spouse's relationship with the children. I'm joking, right? Wrong. Do this by saying nice things about your ex in front of your kids. Don't undermine your ex's authority. Coordinate discipline whenever possible. Keep each other informed about important matters such as homework, school problems, health concerns, etc. Be flexible with your ex's schedule when possible. Don't fight in front of the kids.

Establish a harmonious relationship with your ex after the divorce. Polite tolerance is far better than open hostility. But if you want your kids to suffer less, you and your ex need to learn to be friendly. If that prospect is unnerving, consider this: Parents who are unable to deal respectfully with their former spouses also show less competence, nurturing, and warmth toward their children.

DON'TS

Don't confuse frequency of visitation with quality. Parents do best when they display a combination of warmth plus authority. Permissiveness (warmth but no authority) or domination (authority but no warmth) will make your time together a minus for your kids.

Don't relocate far from your kids. This is essential. Parents who move out of state and start a new life make it impossible for their children to see them or their other parents regularly. Unless one parent is abusive or otherwise incompetent, your child is not served in this situation. In fact, you are increasing the odds that your child's adjustment will be more difficult and prolonged.

A friend of mine from Massachusetts was divorced. His wife remarried and moved to California with their three children. He quit his job and moved to California, too. Later the woman's husband was transferred to New England. My friend quit his job and moved back east to be near his kids. That's called being a father.

Don't let your new marriage interfere with time for your kids. You are obligated to your children. Even if you create more children in your new marriage, you are obligated to your oldest kids. Have alone-time with them once in a while, as well as group-time, even if you have a new family.

Divorce is painful for all involved. Many parents engage in understandable wishful thinking, hoping their kids will emerge healthy and happy from a divorce as long as the parents remain sensitive to their children's feelings. Unfortunately, many parents are so overwhelmed by the difficult process of separation and divorce that they misjudge their children's ability to bounce back. Don't make the mistake of minimizing the effect of divorce and ignoring your children's psychological adjustment. It is an added burden for you at a time when you are already burdened, but your kids will thank you for it later.

PART TWO
mistakes of the body

8

get out of my way. I'm busy!

Does this sound like your life?

You arrive home from a busy but rewarding day at a well-paying job. The house is clean, while the scents of lilacs, cinnamon bread, and a hint of furniture polish waft through the air. Your spouse has arrived ahead of you and is now playing happily with the kids while a wholesome meal is baking in the oven. You have time to take a leisurely shower, or browse through your favorite magazine, or chat on the phone with your best friend from Milwaukee. After a pleasant dinner filled with interesting conversation, the family goes on a short bike ride together (wearing matching helmets). Later, you help the kids with the intricacies of their long-division homework (they are, of course, attentive and appreciative) while your spouse pulls a few of those pesky weeds from your award-winning flower garden. The children go to bed early so that you have time to read them a story and help them say their prayers. Now you and your spouse have an hour or two of quality time together. You talk about your day, your plans, your dreams—all the while your partner is massaging your back—then you engage in a passionate session of lovemaking. It's the third time this week you've made love and you eagerly anticipate tomorrow night . . .

I didn't think it sounded like your life. Instead, many people's lives seem like scenes from a Stephen King novel (including sleeping with a partner who makes deep-throated growls that sound not-quite human).

∾ rearrange your priorities starting today

American couples are on overload. Taking care of little children is a busy job by itself, but more than 60 percent of young mothers are also employed (and employed moms still do more housework and child care than do dads). People have multiple roles to fill—that of spouse, parent, caretaker to aging parents, employee, community volunteer (Girl Scouts, Little League coach, volunteer fire-fighter, Sunday school, and so on), friend, and neighbor. Kids are involved in more extracurricular activities than ever before, requiring Mom or Dad to acquire a chauffeur's license. More adults these days are also trying to squeeze in extra time for exercise (because they can't squeeze into their jeans). And many are spending extra time online—buying, selling, browsing, or chatting.

Home life has grown more hectic and less rewarding. Eating out is convenient and popular, while a leisurely family meal has become a black-and-white photograph from a bygone era. So many couples have embraced the popular myth that it's possible to do it all, and they don't know how they can stop living too close to the edge.

Consequences of Role Overload

Multiple roles sometimes serve as a buffer when stress builds. A warm, loving relationship can soothe the frustrations of a stressful job, for example. But usually this buffering effect peaks quickly and soon you realize you simply have too many responsibilities, not enough help, not enough rest and relaxation, and a growing negative attitude. (The biggest threat to a satisfying sex life? Fatigue.) There are two key consequences to role overload.

REDUCED COUPLE TIME

Since the 1980s, women are working an extra twelve hours per week. Men are working more hours, too. Most of that time comes at the expense of the couple's relationship. In one-quarter of two-income homes the partners work different shifts, which results in less sleep, fewer friends, poorer health, and practically no leisure time together. Sacrificing time with your partner is a mistake that unfolds like this:

- Too busy, the couple puts their relationship on the back burner.
- Over time, they grow more distant.
- This distance causes crankiness—each one feels unappreciated or neglected but fails to see how they are not giving enough to the other.
- This crankiness makes any time together less satisfying.
- Then they devote more time to the kids or the job, thereby adding to their distance.

There is no such thing as a good, strong family if the couple's relationship is weak.

Soon they have adapted to the situation. Alone time with the partner feels awkward or is marred by tension. They have little to talk about. Efforts to force good feelings ("Let's do something fun . . .") are halfhearted and easily derailed. So what do they do? Spend more time at work, or with the kids, or at the gym—and the couple's relationship continues to suffer.

ROLE CONFUSION

Who does what in the relationship? This is less of a problem for a cohabiting couple. Often, responsibilities for chores are clear-cut, and there is a greater tendency for each to do his or her fair share. This seems equitable but occurs mostly because cohabiting couples maintain a greater sense of independence from each other. Married couples expect more. When premarital expectations do not match the reality of marital life, depression emerges, arguments ensue, and it becomes more difficult to balance career, family, and personal obligations.

Men are doing more house and baby-care chores than ever before (triple the amount since the 1960s). However, in dual-career households, women still do more of the housework and child care than men do. "I'm the director of maintenance and recreation," one mother said. "I just wish my husband would take that job over once in a while." Women also do more of the "emotional work" of the family: caring for a child's emotional needs and for the expressiveness of the couple's relationship. If a parent has to get up in the middle of the night for a sick child, or take time off from work to take the child to a pediatric appointment, or to have a parent-teacher conference, that parent is more often the mother.

Confusion over roles and responsibilities is due, in part, to the fact that men and women haven't completely shed traditional role stereotypes, yet they live in a society that insists that they do. Tradition holds that men focus most on providing and protecting their families. Men therefore place work at the center of their lives. Tradition holds that women focus on nurturing the spouse and children and making sure that hour-to-hour needs are met. Women therefore place the family at the center of their lives. These stereotypes are still true. Despite househusbands and working mothers, despite paternity leave and day-care centers—all of which seem to overturn traditional roles—those old-fashioned roles still beat in the hearts of most people.

Given that most parents work, more kids have to spend some time by themselves after school. Kids home alone after school for more than eleven hours per week are at double the risk of using drugs, alcohol, or cigarettes. Parents need to modify their work schedules or make arrangements for other providers to be available. The negative effects of being home alone are higher for kids in urban areas. Also, junior high girls who "hang out" after school with friends because of lack of parental supervision are more likely to associate with older teens and have a higher chance of getting into trouble than boys their same age.

Don't get me wrong. Women worry about money, too. But men take it personally. When money is tight, men carry that burden on their shoulders, even if their partners work. In the saddest cases, a man works two or three jobs for the sake of his family but is never available to the family he is providing for. Sometimes their partners complain. But is the family willing to get by on substantially less (no cable TV, no computers, and a smaller car) so that Dad can be home at night?

Don't get me wrong. Dads worry about the children, too. But moms take it personally. When the kids are ill, doing poorly in school, or unable to get along with other children, a mom is likely to lose sleep over it.

An often-quoted study involved 139 couples with professional careers. The women in the study were either successful in business or were professors. So were their mates. Despite the obvious presumption that these couples would share equally in housekeeping and child-rearing roles, the women did more (not too surprising, is it?). And yet, these women were very pleased with their partners' participation. But they were displeased with their own. *These women felt they were not doing enough for their children.*

If a mother has to miss her child's school play due to work, she feels like a bad mother. If a father misses the play because of work, he regrets it but feels less guilty. That is because he is much more likely to view working as "doing for my family." Obviously, this is a generalization and there are many exceptions. Still, that is the tendency. The changes in society that allow couples to break free of traditional roles are too new. Men and women have not caught up with the new rules. Perhaps this is due to the fact that most couples were raised in homes where more traditional roles existed.

Stop Juggling and Start Living

You can't fix overload by fine-tuning your life. If your philosophy is to try and have it all, then any cutting back you do will be too little and temporary. You have to be willing to give up something. You can't have it all, and you're better off not trying.

When people want to save money, they are often advised "pay yourself first." That is why employees often have money taken directly from their paychecks for savings or retirement. If they didn't do it that way, they'd spend the money instead of saving it. A married couple must learn to "pay their marriage first." Obviously, children's daily needs cannot be ignored. But putting your marriage on the back burner is a prescription for stress and unhappiness. You can't have a few minutes a day of quality time with your mate and expect passion and devotion to flourish. You must have quantity and quality.

WHAT CAN YOU DO TO FIND THE TIME?

Do your best to stick to a routine with your young children. Inconsistent bed, bath, or dinner times can throw kids off schedule. When a couple shares these responsibilities, it allows each parent extra time to get a much-needed breather. Even a chance to take a longer, undisturbed shower can be refreshing to a harried parent. Or a chance to go grocery shopping without kids might feel like a vacation when parents are on overload.

Say no to low-priority tasks. That means the floor may remain cluttered or the car won't get washed.

Make the mundane a little special. If your dinner is takeout, try to have everyone sit at the table together. Or, bring it outside for a picnic. Letting kids eat while watching TV so you can get a few extra chores done is okay, but should be done sparingly. Why? Because shortcuts to parenting and housework maintain the false illusion that you can do it all and that eating together as a family is unimportant. Eating together is not a cure for wayward kids, but parents who insist that the family eat together often are probably doing more things right.

Have regular or weekly family time. It really does help family functioning. Especially if done weekly, families get into a habit where they simply don't make plans to do anything else at that time. It curtails impulsive decisions, offers predictability, and may be the only time the family sits together for an hour during the week.

In fact, despite time constraints, people in a satisfying marriage find ways to make time for each other. They don't make excuses.

Separate business from family fun time. Parents often try to squeeze in other activities while they are attending to their kids. If you can get the kids to help with dinner or clean up their rooms in a fun way, terrific. But a mom may think about her business presentation while playing a board game, or a dad might be making calls on his cell phone while tossing a ball to his toddler. Parents thus become preoccupied bystanders in their children's lives. Kids who clamor for their parents' attention are likely to clamor less when they know they can count on regular, uninterrupted, meaningful time. But if they are always tugging at your pants because you are busy cooking, cleaning, chatting, or doing business, they will learn to keep tugging as the only way to ensure some attention—or they'll learn they are not worth your time.

Talk about stress with your partner. Couples under high stress who adopt a more masculine philosophy are unhappy. This philosophy contains three main components: restricted expression of emotions; reduced affection; and preoccupation with career success. Talking about stress with your partner can actually improve intimacy.

Examine how hectic your children's lives are. Cut back on their extracurricular activities if need be. Such activities are great and serve a purpose. But many kids are overextended. Day-care or school, plus homework, plus sports, plus Scouts, plus martial arts, plus music or dance lessons, plus playtime with friends . . . when do they have time to play with Mom and Dad?

Drastically reduce TV and computer time. What should be an enjoyable break from stress often takes over as a mild addiction or tranquilizer. When TV time is drastically reduced, kids get more homework done, read more, have more time for other physical and creative activities, and so do you. TV time was meant to be a cure for stress. It has become part of the problem.

9

we're not
newlyweds anymore

When you love someone but don't show it with thoughtful words or gestures, it can create doubt in your partner's mind. For the healthiest couples, this is often corrected just by calling attention to the situation. But for average couples with their share of stresses or unresolved hurts, this issue can blossom into a stubborn standoff.

"You don't love me."

"Of course I do. Look at all the things I've done for you. Don't you realize how much work I've put into the new bathroom?"

"That doesn't count. Why do you always think you are Mr. Wonderful just because you fix things around the house? When was the last time you told me you loved me? When was the last time you just wanted to hold my hand and go for a walk?"

"If I didn't love you I wouldn't bother working so hard around here."

"You just don't get it."

"No. *You* don't get it."

It's a common mistake for couples in love to skimp on appreciation, compliments, and affection. And then they wonder why their partner is such a grump in the morning.

∾ cherish your mate and *show* you mean it

All couples will take each other for granted. It's human nature. The more serious mistake occurs when neglect reaches a level where your partner seriously doubts your love. He or she no longer feels special or cherished. In over fifteen years of being a marriage therapist, I've come to view cherishing and being cherished as a fundamental ingredient for a happy, successful relationship. If you or your partner don't feel cherished, your relationship will unravel. And it will take more than a few kind words or thoughtful gestures to fix things.

The irony is that when you feel cherished you can handle the occasional lapses in attention or affection. You can put up with being taken for granted. You will give your partner the benefit of the doubt ("He's been so tired . . . She's been working so hard . . . He has so much on his mind . . . ") and trust that very soon your partner's gaze will be on you.

From Getting Along to Cherishing

The last time I saw Walt and Libby, their marriage had improved significantly. They had halted their frequent criticisms, talked more, and spent more time together. But I was uneasy because I never sensed that they really cherished one another. So I was surprised when I met Libby in a parking lot two years later and she told me how wonderful her marriage was. I saw the sparkle in her eyes when she spoke about Walt and the sense of genuine peace that surrounded her like a light. I wondered how they had finally learned to cherish one another.

Then I noticed her bandanna and the very thin hair it almost covered. Libby was dying from cancer. Her illness had propelled the couple's relationship to a higher and more spiritual level. They saw each other as precious gifts and treated each other accordingly. When I read her obituary six weeks later, I knew that Walt had lost the person he cherished most in this world.

Getting along and not taking each other for granted is important. But it's not enough. It's like climbing a tall mountain but turning back just when the summit is in reach. It's great that you made it that far, but why did you stop?

People hold back from truly cherishing their mate for three common reasons.

1. *Getting bogged down.* Day-to-day hassles, job stress, poor health, and too little time together put the couple in the proverbial rut. If caught early,

couples can climb out of the rut. Otherwise, they sink deeper into it and the next major factor unfolds.

2. *Resentments develop.* Each partner begins to feel entitled to love and attention and is angry that they are not receiving it. A vicious cycle develops where neither partner can fully give to the other until they get something first. If this persists, partners doubt how much they love or are loved. Commonly, partners pursue other interests as a defense against being hurt. So they work more hours, spend more time separately with the kids, or more time away from home.

3. *Old wounds surface.* The more a person was hurt by their parents or by previous lovers, the harder it will be to truly devote themselves to their partner. They will want to, but they'll also be afraid to (or will overdo it in a smothering way). When this is happening, relationships tend to be herky-jerky. There is a pattern of getting close and backing away.

> *When your mate is irritable, tired, and hard to approach, don't automatically give space. Your partner may be feeling neglected. If so, show your love and attention.*

We are creatures of habit. The longer a pattern of neglect persists, the more it will continue to persist. And it may be difficult to recognize the pattern because it is so much a part of how we behave. It's like a room that needs repainting or a doorway with a broken piece of molding. After a while we don't notice it, so it remains in a state of disrepair.

Clues to "Relationship Neglect"

Neglect occurs gradually, so gradually that you don't notice it at first. If called to your attention, you make excuses. You think things such as:

She knows I love her. (Oh? How does she know?)

So what if I don't call him at work anymore. He doesn't mind. He's too busy anyway. (Are you sure? Maybe he just isn't saying anything about it.)

If it bothered her, she'd say something. (Maybe. Maybe not.)

He doesn't care about such things. (Maybe he stopped caring because he had no choice.)

What's the big deal? We're not newlyweds anymore. (The honeymoon is a state of mind.)

In recent months or years, have you:

- Started going to bed earlier or later than your mate?
- Made more decisions by yourself that in the past you would discuss?
- Cut back on calling her at work just to say hi?
- Stopped telling her how good she looks?
- Cared less and less about your appearance?
- Spent more quality time with friends or coworkers than your partner?
- Been more critical, especially over little things, while ignoring all the good stuff?
- Preferred much more quality time with your computer or TV instead of your mate?
- Viewed your partner as less sexy?
- Ignored each other when you had an unexpected hour without the kids?
- Made love more mechanically rather than enthusiastically?
- Looked forward to coming home so that you can flop on the couch?

If you answered yes to five or fewer, you are in a rut but can probably climb your way out with a little effort. If you answered yes to between six and nine, you are not only in a rut, you are resentful. But your mate is resenting you, too. Your best bet is not to blame your partner but start changing your ways while encouraging your mate to do the same. If you answered yes to more than nine, you are likely very unhappy. Change is certainly possible, but it might take more than good intentions. A relationship workshop or a weekend getaway might spark some changes, but sessions with a therapist might also be required.

Just What Does It Mean to Be Cherished?

Cherishing is not romance. It can include romance, but romance isn't required. You can be romantic with someone you just met, but you won't cherish that person. Cherishing your mate transcends the physical. Still, a partner who wants more romance from her mate probably wants to feel deeply loved and treasured. A radiant look into your partner's eyes or a tender embrace may be more significant than roses or a walk on the beach.

Cherishing is certainly an aspect of loving, but it is an enhanced form of love, an aspect that is both brighter and deeper. Being beloved feels different than being loved. It contains that extra ingredient that can make the difference between a relationship that survives and one that thrives.

How to Climb Out of the Rut

It takes more than desire. Couples get into ruts all the time despite good intentions because they allow their feelings to take precedence over their actions. *Feeling* love becomes good enough, instead of *showing* love. (Or feeling angry or tired is reason enough to stop showing love.)

It's essential that you show love in a way that matters to your partner. A friendly phone call during the day might be a welcome surprise. Then again, leaving wet towels on the floor after your morning shower may not arouse much appreciation. It's an overgeneralization, but often true, that men show they care by doing certain tasks such as fixing the VCR or painting the garage. What they don't do enough of is say "I love you" or hold their partner's hand while strolling in the mall. Women may say sweet things to their partner, but what really might matter to him is a ham sandwich while he watches the ballgame or a warm hug after a long, tiresome day at work. You won't know for sure unless you ask, "What could I do that would make you feel more loved?"

Some tips can get the process moving. Try these ideas for several weeks. Be creative. Don't slack off because you're tired or preoccupied. No excuses!

- Each of you must initiate nonsexual affection at least four times a day. If you want to get grabby and playful, fine. But that doesn't count toward the required four.
- Get out the photo album and start reminiscing. You don't have to plan this. Just start looking at old photos and say, "Oh, honey, look at this! You're so much better looking now than you were then." He'll get curious, and chances are you'll get each other hooked.
- Say wonderful things about your mate to your friends or family.
- Discuss your day, or the bills, or your child's upcoming birthday while giving each other a massage. Maybe you can each lie on opposite ends of the couch and rub each other's feet. The idea is to make ordinary conversations a bit more special.
- Step outside for a few minutes before bed. Hold each other while looking at the stars or talking about tomorrow's plans.
- Make a lunch date.
- For a week, leave notes mentioning one thing you admire or appreciate about each other. It doesn't have to be profound. "You always play so well with the kids" is a nice and worthy sentiment.

- Book a baby-sitter for eight Friday nights (or any night) in a row. Even if you can't afford dinner, go and have coffee together.
- Always kiss goodnight and good morning. Always kiss when you see each other at the end of the day.

Most people learn to get by on less than they'd like in a relationship. But that leaves little wiggle room if the relationship hits a rough spot. Besides, anybody who is "getting by" in their most significant relationship is lonelier for it. Don't be someone who makes his or her partner feel lonely. Find ways to show appreciation and not take each other for granted. If you persevere, you may discover that you are not only tolerated, you are loved. And not only loved, you are cherished.

10
I promise, it'll never happen again

"I don't trust him," Fran said about her fiancé. They had been living together for about fifteen months. The wedding was six months away. Was Dan unfaithful? No. Did he engage in criminal or unsavory activity? No. Fran mistrusted Dan because he did not keep his promises. When someone questions a partner's trustworthiness, the likelihood is that sexual faithfulness is not the issue, although infidelity shatters trust and is a devastating blow to a relationship. (See chapter 15 for that discussion.)

Dan was a nice guy. He just wasn't reliable. It began with his tendency to cancel plans he had with Fran at the last minute. Business was his excuse. But he rarely seemed to miss his spring games in the softball league. Then there were the house repairs that he'd start but never finish. And the promise to take Fran on a romantic vacation—at least a weekend or two of fun and frivolity. She'd bring up the topic, he'd say let's do it, but he'd hesitate in setting a specific date. To make matters worse, she'd caught him in a few lies. Not big ones. Mostly he was trying to fib his way through some poor excuses for not keeping his promises. He'd downplay his faults and insinuate that Fran was becoming intolerant and hard to satisfy. Red flags were waving in front of Fran. Was this the guy she should trust with her future and her children's future? Should she postpone the wedding?

People like Dan who would never cheat on their mate still make careless mistakes in the area of trust, sometimes without realizing it.

You question the degree of trust in your relationship (even when you believe your partner is sexually faithful) when you start to worry:

Why isn't my partner reliable?

Why doesn't he always speak the truth?

Why is it hard to be myself with this person?

Why does my partner flirt or ignore me when we're with others?

ᴏᴠ **keep your promises and be trustworthy**

Trust is truly the foundation of any meaningful, lasting relationship. Trust is weakened when:

- Your partner is unreliable, making promises that are well-intended but often not kept.

- Your partner is sharply critical, "flies off the handle," tends to blame you when things go wrong while he is always "right," or is inattentive. You will not speak your mind as easily when you cannot trust that you will be listened to or understood.

- One of you routinely emphasizes personal pursuits at the expense of the other's needs. Maybe she buys the latest computer when you already have too many bills. Maybe he visits his family every weekend when you already have insufficient time alone together. Reliability means knowing that your needs will be considered when your partner makes decisions.

- One of you lies, even about little things that could easily have been addressed truthfully.

- You've been betrayed by others in the past and are quick to judge now. (Adults whose parents fought openly and harshly have a tendency to grow up with less trust in the benevolence of others.)

- One of you is pursued by an ex-partner but doesn't do much to stop it.

Without trust, all the other essential ingredients become weakened. For example, intimacy is a vital ingredient. Intimacy is the ability to be vulnerable with your partner, to share dreams, and to bond during adversity. But you can't bare your soul to someone who might use what you say against you. You will hold back and begin living a life that is more private than intimate.

Mistrust weakens commitment. If you are unmarried, you will have serious reservations about tying the knot. If you are already married, you will wonder if you've made a mistake. You may fantasize about leaving. A chain reaction is set off whereby your mistrust breeds tension or emotional distance that can further corrode the relationship and add more mistrust.

Jealousy: Is It Ever a Good Thing?

Jealousy is a paradox. It can prod a couple into greater commitment and passion, or it can divide a couple. Phil attended his wife Janet's twentieth high school reunion. Janet's senior prom date seemed thrilled to see her after so many years and embraced her fiercely. It made Phil's stomach tighten. He was not worried about his relationship, but the sight of another man fawning over his wife made him feel jealous. He never mentioned his insecurity. Later that night he and Janet made passionate love.

But imagine that same scene occurring in the context of a strained marriage. Maybe Janet had begun to complain that Phil spent more and more time at work or with his friends than with her. Or maybe Phil was growing aggravated over a decline in their sex life. Or maybe Janet had even mentioned the word *divorce* in one of their conversations. Now the scene at the high school reunion can take on extra meaning. It might be viewed as more of a threat and could result in a nasty argument later on.

Some view jealousy as an immature reaction that reveals personal insecurity. A jealous man may be branded as "possessive" or "controlling." A jealous woman might be regarded as "dependent" or "hysterical." However, according to David Buss's book *Dangerous Passion*, partners sometimes elicit jealousy out of love, as a way to test the strength of the relationship. Smiling for an extra split second at someone of the opposite sex—in full view of one's mate—or ignoring a partner at a social gathering are tactics people sometimes use. Women tend to purposely elicit jealousy twice as often as men. And they do so about 40 percent of the time as a reminder to their partners that greener pastures are available should his attentiveness or commitment dissipate. Such provocations can serve to crank up a sluggish relationship and allow partners to not take each other for granted. But done too often or to an extreme, it can lead to mistrust and accusations of unfaithfulness.

If jealousy is becoming a problem in your relationship, use the following guidelines:

- Pathological jealousy requires professional help. A jealous partner who insists that you should rarely go out, who limits your spending, or who expects you to account for every minute of your time is abusive and only fueling their own jealous beliefs. The partner is creating a situation whereby the only way he or she can trust you is to limit you. That's not trust. That's a prison.

- Minor jealousies should not be a reason to argue. Instead, see them as signs of a mild insecurity and discuss this insecurity with your partner. Don't focus on what your partner did to make you jealous ("You kept putting your arm around his neck whenever he made you laugh."). Your partner may accuse you of overreacting and you'll get into a no-win debate. Instead, look at ways you feel insecure in the relationship and discuss what needs to happen to improve your trust. ("I guess what really bothered me was that you seemed to have fun with him. We don't have fun like that when we do things. I'd like us to go somewhere and have a great time together.")

- Evoking jealousy is more common when dating. Don't automatically assume that such a partner cannot be trusted. He or she might just be testing you. It isn't fatal and may well be a sign that your partner is interested in you.

- If your former mate betrayed you, your new partner should not pay the price. Don't say, "If you loved me you wouldn't do . . . because that makes me insecure." Your partner's actions may be reasonable and to expect to curtail them is unfair. Unfair mistrust breeds resentment.

- Don't go out of your way to incite jealousy, particularly if your partner has expressed concern. Making a partner jealous is a little like playing with fire. Sometimes it sheds light, sometimes somebody gets burned.

The Unreliable Partner

The partner who makes promises but doesn't always keep them is making the serious mistake of taking his partner's trust in him for granted. But sometimes failed promises are really miscalculations or miscommunications.

Before you complain (again) about your mate's unreliability, look at all the factors.

> *Sometimes an unreliable partner is an overextended partner or perhaps an under-appreciated partner who loses the enthusiasm to follow through.*

- Is your partner stressed or spread too thin by too many responsibilities?
- Have your condemnations backfired and made cooperation less likely?
- Did you have a clear understanding of what was expected or did you both miscommunicate?
- Are there recurrent complaints about you that have not been corrected?
- Are you a demanding person in general?

In clinical practice, unreliability is due to one of two reasons:

1. *Serious disturbances* such as alcoholism or gambling, or flagrant immaturity. Until that person matures or gets help for their addiction, not much will change.
2. *Mild stylistic differences* (he's a bit of a perfectionist, she's not; she likes the novelty of change, he prefers the status quo; he always finds busywork, she likes time to relax; and so on). These become inflamed over time as each person tries to get the other to change. This results in a standoff and an undercurrent of ill will, which makes cooperation and understanding less likely.

If you think you and your mate fall into the second category, then changing your pattern of responding and using a softer touch will pay dividends. Realize that you may have to accept some differences and learn to live with them, but that partners are more willing to sacrifice for each other and compromise if they feel respected, cared about, and understood. Negotiation can help, too. If your partner tends to run late for things, agree to take separate cars if waiting will make you late to an important function. Don't argue or complain, just do it. If she is a do-it-yourselfer but your home is constantly under construction and never completed, agree that past a certain point you will hire someone to finish the job. If he doesn't care for the kids in the way that you would (he doesn't dress or feed them "adequately"; he seems lax on supervision), don't automatically run in to correct him. He might take offense or he might let you take over, which is in nobody's best interest. On average, dads are less particular about things than moms when it comes to child care. Moms want the outfits to match; dads don't care. Moms may jump in when the kids are fighting; dads may hold off until someone starts screaming bloody murder. It's a mistake for partners to argue that their way is right and their partner's way is wrong. It's better to say, "I know your way works for you, but I'd feel better if you'd do it this way. Do you mind?" That shows respect. It's also better to ignore some things.

An unreliable partner corrodes trust. But don't be too quick to assume it's your partner's entire fault. You may have unwittingly added to the problem by your own personality style, your own misunderstandings, or your need to have things go your way. If you make some corrections and then ask your partner to do the same, you may discover that your mate is more reliable than you thought.

Lying: The Painful Truth

Lies happen. In one survey, adults admitted to lying about thirteen times a week. However, most of those lies were "white lies" said to protect someone's feelings. Sometimes people lie about small things because they want to avoid an argument. A man might lie about the cost of a lawn mower because he knew his wife would be upset. A woman might lie about spending an afternoon with a friend if she knows that her partner didn't like that friend. These lies may not cause problems. They may even remain undetected. But they are not insignificant. At best, they are a method of coping used because more forthright methods don't work. At worst, they can undermine faith in one's partner. No one likes to be lied to. But most people don't like having to lie, either.

Frequent lies are much more serious. A frequent liar makes their partner go crazy. Even an occasional liar makes their partner have to second-guess them in an exhausting effort to determine the truth. Liars rarely confess when first confronted. So mistrustful partners have to figure out what to believe: their own intuition or their mate's proclamation of innocence. When a lie is eventually exposed and the liar has to admit the truth, their partners are often more disturbed by the agony they had to go through when they didn't know what to believe, than they are disturbed by the lie. A lie can be forgiven, perhaps even understood as an effort to cover up an infraction that, if exposed, would send the relationship into a tailspin. But a persistent lie, in the face of pleas to be honest, shreds a partner's sense of reality and security. So why does the partner repeatedly lie despite its negative effects on the other person? The answer to that question, though harsh, is usually true: The lying partner did not care enough about his partner's emotional well-being.

If your partner is a persistent liar, then your relationship is being held together more by fear and a sense of personal inadequacy than by love. Probably, you fear losing your mate and are afraid you will not attract someone better. Or you fear what will happen to you or to your children financially. But there is no trust, and you cannot sleep easily. These relationships are always unhappy. Most don't survive.

When you care about your partner, you will not abuse his or her faith in you. Fractured trust makes the relationship vulnerable. A relationship with a solid foundation of trust can weather most storms.

11

if you love me,
you'll *show* me

Couples in a long-term relationship often get into a pattern where they regard affection and foreplay the same way they might open a wrapped birthday present: The woman admires the design of the wrapping, caresses the package, slides her fingers gently under the folded ends to slip off the tape, removes the wrapping carefully—being sure not to tear it needlessly—lays aside the ribbon while remarking how pretty it is, and finally exposes the gift underneath.

A man just rips off the wrapping to get to the box.

While a hurried effort at sex might be playful and appealing once in a while, men make the mistake of neglecting or at least minimizing foreplay and displays of nonsexual affection. The result is that women feel more beleaguered than beloved, more a piece of meat than a mate. Eventually, she views his invitations to sex as self-serving. He's only after one thing. This sentiment is particularly common when the woman feels neglected in general. It's nice to know that her mate is attracted to her body, but without daily tender affection or frequent thoughtful gestures, she doesn't feel special. Instead, she believes she's a sperm bank holding on to his deposit. Hardly the stuff of romance. Men make the mistake of underestimating the importance of affection to women and are too quick to push for sex.

But women make the mistake of misunderstanding the true meaning of sex to men. Women in a long-term relationship often pull away from sex when the men are unaffectionate, which only increases men's sexual desire and need for sexual closeness.

For newly dating couples, sex often occurs before the couple really knows each other or is committed to one another. But it forces a pseudo-intimacy since genuine intimacy takes time. If a person is trying to find a permanent partner, sex too soon may not be wise. According to the most recent findings from a scientific survey of American's sexual behavior, delaying sex for at least a year gives you the best odds of future marriage. The survey showed that 55 percent of couples who eventually married waited a year or more before having sex—"reflecting in part the choice among many couples to abstain from sex until marriage"; only 10 percent of couples who had sex within the first month of dating ended up married. The reverse is true for cohabiting couples. About 36 percent had sex within a month, and after a year or more, all but 16 percent had sex. Interestingly, the divorce rate for cohabiting couples who eventually married was nearly twice that of non-cohabiting couples who married. And the divorce rate when at least one partner was a virgin at the time of marriage is estimated at less than half the average divorce rate for couples who were not virgins at the time of the wedding.

∾ first develop intimacy and show nonsexual affection

Kyle and Mary had been dating for about a month. Kyle was looking for a meaningful relationship and his intuition told him that Mary might be the woman for him. Unlike past relationships where he pursued quickly for sex, Kyle held back this time.

"I know she expected me to want to go to bed with her. And I do want to. But I also want her to know I respect her."

What confused him was Mary's reaction. "Aren't you attracted to me?" she asked. "Why haven't you tried to have sex with me yet?"

The irony is that Mary wasn't interested in sex for the sake of sex. She, too, wanted a relationship that held the promise of a future together. Had Kyle made a sexual move earlier, she would have resisted it. But when he held back, she became confused and worried and took on the role of sexual pursuer.

Researchers often study college students to gain insight into the human condition. (Unfortunately, students are about as representative of the adult population as are lab rats.) According to one survey, male students expect to have sex after about ten dates. Women students expect sex after about fifteen dates. Since students define a date as simply "hanging out together," they reach the required quota of dates in about three weeks or less. In these cases, getting physical is not about love and marriage. It's more about sexual experimentation and learning about relationships. These students are less interested in finding a mate than they are in mating who they find.

People who have had too many relationship failures are sometimes more likely to engage in sex prematurely as a way of hedging their bets—inviting closeness so as to pretend that their relationship is meaningful. But sex alone does not make it meaningful. Only true devotion does that.

But what about older, more mature people? Such couples often have sex by around the sixth date, though there is wide variability. Women in their late twenties or early thirties sometimes give in to sex earlier in a relationship, paradoxically decreasing the odds of marriage with that partner. People who have unhitched themselves from a former mate and are accustomed to having sex on a regular basis tend to have sex earlier in their new dating relationship.

Once intimacy is in place, sex might improve closeness, but it might also complicate the relationship, especially if it results in an unwanted pregnancy.

It's Okay to Take Your Time

In a survey of women ages seventeen to thirty-five, the timing of the first sexual intercourse with a new partner was associated with the perception of increased commitment. Women had sex more often when they believed the man was committed to them. The same women rated sex without commitment as less acceptable.

In general, the problem for many women who crave commitment is that they misjudge a man's intent. Men are more willing to have sex without commitment. So by having sex too soon, many well-intended women make the men feel trapped and drive them away.

Most people give in to sex early on because it is recreational (they do it for themselves, not for the relationship), or they believe (rightly in many cases) that their partner will dump them if they don't. Some men don't feel masculine if they delay having sex. But sex without the deeper intimacy, which can only come from meaningful (nonsexual) time together and a commitment to one another, makes for a lopsided and potentially unstable relationship. The relationship (usually) heads off in a direction that is primarily sexual. Emotional intimacy is secondary.

In too many relationships, sex without love or commitment is also degrading (we become objects—things to use—not a person with a heart and soul). Those may seem like old-fashioned words, but deep down most people want sex to mean much more than the price paid for several dates or the price paid to avoid loneliness.

Too many people with good hearts and bountiful dreams jump into bed with someone they like a lot, only to find that the relationship ends quickly thereafter (this is a common complaint of women). They not only feel rejected, they often feel humiliated. They gave their heart and their body to a person they hoped would treasure it, and instead their body was abandoned.

RULES OF THUMB FOR DATING COUPLES

- Focus on developing emotional intimacy. This comes from getting to know each other's dreams, values, backgrounds, and style of behavior. Be friends first.
- Show lots of affection as your fondness for the other person grows.
- If your partner is pushing for sex and you're not ready, try to openly discuss your concerns with your partner.
- If your partner still pushes for sex and gives you an ultimatum, walk away. If your partner really does love you, he or she will want you back and will learn to respect your wishes. Be brave, and you might be able to build the relationship you want.
- Once you start a sexual relationship, pay attention to signs. Is your partner acting more committed to you? Good! But does that scare you and make you want to pull away? Is your partner withdrawing? If so, sex might have come too soon. Rate what you believe is your partner's investment in this relationship from zero (not invested at all) to ten (he wants to marry you and would die for you). Now rate your investment. If you are more than two points away from your mate, chances are that the relationship is uneven and one of you will be more anxious about trying to keep it going. Having sex won't help in that situation. It only gives you the illusion of

closeness. The partner who is more invested needs to tone it down. It may be hard, but it is necessary to prevent the more invested person from carrying the weight of the relationship and getting burned in the end.

The Long-Term Couple

In long-term relationships, men and women often misunderstand what sex and affection mean to their partners. It is perhaps the most common mistake couples make. Women tend to underestimate how important it is to a man to make love (no, he isn't just after sex), and men underestimate the importance of affection to women (no, it isn't a signal from her that she wants sex).

In a committed relationship, men need to make love in order to feel deeply loved. They may know intellectually that they are loved, but they *feel* loved when they make love. (It is perhaps a primitive way of responding, but most men can't help it.)

Despite his clumsy way of showing it, a man in a committed relationship who pushes for sex isn't just craving an orgasm. Instead, he wants reassurance that he is deeply loved.

On the other hand, women need thoughtfulness, affection, and love in order to feel fully sexual.

This difference doesn't matter in happy, thriving marriages because each side gets what they need. But when tension is high or misunderstandings and hurts have accumulated, this difference starts to affect a relationship. At such times, men often pursue sex so they can reassure themselves that they are loved. But they do so with little regard for showing tender affection (seeing it as the equivalent of lacing up their sneakers before barreling out onto the basketball court for the big match). If they do show affection, it is more poking and prodding of a sexual nature, not the warm kind that tells a woman she is cherished.

A man in a committed relationship pushes for sex as a way to invite closeness. A woman may say no to sex as a way to invite affection and closeness. Men and women often want the same thing—emotional closeness—but they go about it in different ways.

When a relationship is strained but not quite to the breaking point, a woman views her man's genital-obsession as a sign that he is an adolescent at heart. So she pulls back from sex, craving instead intimate talks, mature romance, and affection. The man feels rejected once again, certainly puzzled. He backs off from sex and believes he is showing patience and respect for her wishes, though he doesn't understand those wishes. After a period of time, he comes into close proximity of his beloved other (ten feet is usually close enough), he reads her body language (blinking; a dry, hacking cough), and decides she is finally inviting him to have sex—a clear case of delusional thinking. He vigorously grabs her once again, and makes the same tactical blunder.

RULES OF THUMB FOR COUPLES
IN A COMMITTED RELATIONSHIP

- Men must learn to show nonsexual affection on a daily basis. Also, converse a bit more often and add to your frequency of thoughtful gestures. It is what your partner truly needs and is the most effective way to increase the frequency of sex.
- Women must learn that withholding sex as a method to teach their mate to be affectionate is misguided. If your mate doubts that you love him, he may push for more sex and sidestep affection. Let him know in your intimate moments just how much his affection (nonsexual) means to you.
- If the woman has been feeling particularly hurt and unloved for quite some time, engaging in sex will feel cheap. But withholding sex adds to the man's frustration. The best bet is for each to realize the vicious cycle. The man should show frequent nonsexual affection—not to earn points for sex, but to reveal his love and caring for her. The woman should respond affectionately and without critical comments. Within a month (*You're kidding! That long?* Yes, that long . . .), if the woman feels that the man was making a sincere effort, she should let him know what he means to her. Hopefully, each will realize that tender shows of affection and lovemaking are the two pillars of sexual intimacy.
- Once in a while, engage in sex without orgasm. It teaches appreciation for the sometimes-overlooked facets of sexual play, and the time together is likely to last longer than it would if orgasm was the outcome. Besides, it makes reaching orgasm next time all the more enjoyable.

When it comes to wanting a healthy, loving, intimate, committed relationship with someone you can trust, don't be stupid. Don't let your genitals do your thinking. The best approach is to postpone sex until the relationship is a fully committed one. It isn't always what friends or the media recommend, but it's smart.

12

I refuse to talk about this right now

The best predictor of whether a relationship will succeed or fail is how well the couple manages conflict. The more criticism, defensiveness, or withdrawal there is, the more likely the relationship will be unsatisfying and potentially doomed. These three factors show up in every relationship. But their effects can be minimized if the couple gets along most of the time and does not harbor ill will.

Most people know instinctively that criticisms, put-downs, and a tendency to blame will lead to defensiveness, arguments, or emotional distance. Yet couples in conflict do these all the time. The mistake is really twofold:

1. One or both members have a tendency to find fault. Or, one or both have a tendency to act in ways that provoke criticism (he leaves a mess wherever he goes, she seems hard to satisfy, and so on). They know that such behaviors rarely produce positive results, yet they do them anyway.

2. As conflicts go unresolved, partners do even *more* blaming, defending, or withdrawing. Like having a car stuck in the mud, these partners press on the accelerator and inflame the conflict. But avoiding conflict

by withdrawing is as troublesome as provoking conflict by criticizing. The conflict-avoider may feel that he is taking the moral high ground (conflict-avoiders are almost always male), but he is contributing to the perpetuation of the problem because he is not addressing any concerns. He just wants to avoid an argument. Meanwhile, his partner is feeling ignored, taken for granted, or frustrated by his unwillingness to participate in a problem-solving conversation.

At this phase, attitudes and perceptions become negative and hardened. Each one views the other as more of the problem, so each sticks to their guns. Criticisms may subside from time to time, but they will flare up again soon, usually over little things. That only prompts return-fire or else the other partner shuts down.

It's a vicious cycle: Men withdraw to avoid arguments, and women criticize their men for withdrawing.

The criticize-withdraw pattern is the most common one in couples and it is self-perpetuating. It is no surprise, therefore, that the primary complaint women have of men is, "He won't communicate," while a typical complaint of men is, "When I do speak up, all I get is grief!"

∾ face difficult discussions, don't avoid them

Esteemed researcher Dr. John Gottman makes a distinction between complaints and criticisms. Complaints are less personal. They are not attacks but an expression of dissatisfaction. "We don't get out much anymore" is a complaint. "You're more interested in the TV than you are me" is a criticism. Often, complaints are easier to hear because no one is being singled out for blame. But when complaints get ignored or discussions fall apart, complaints degrade into criticisms—which sometimes makes things worse.

But trying to complain without criticizing, or trying to sidestep an argument without withdrawing, is not that simple. In fact, most couples have tried many times to say or do the right thing, only to have it backfire. Pamela and Paul often fell into this trap. Paul believed that Pam's style was a bit smothering. She had an opinion about many things, and since her opinions differed from his, he felt criticized. Pam just enjoyed conversation and was frustrated by his need to have time away from her. She wished he was more intimate, more of a companion. He wished she'd leave him alone to clear his head once in a while and say things more sweetly. From time to time, each one tried to cooperate by suppressing any troublesome behavior. He would strike up a conversation or follow her around the house when he really felt like sticking earphones on his head and listening to music. And she'd be sure to give him space and not try to coax him out of his cave when he looked like he needed time to be alone.

> For real change to occur, both sides must change. However, the one who avoids intimacy more or who withdraws more (usually the male) must be willing to make more effort to change.

The problem is that *not* pursuing, *not* criticizing, and *not* withdrawing is *not* so obvious. Paul might not notice when Pam is leaving him alone. In fact, he may think she is just busy with other things and not give her credit for trying. Pam might notice when Paul speaks up and spends more time with her; but then again she might not. After all, Paul doesn't always ignore her. After a few days of giving Paul his space, and after a few days where Paul tries to talk more, each feels entitled to get more of what they want. So when Pam requests that she and Paul go out for an evening or just take a walk (she's entitled to more intimacy), he might feel enough is enough and say "Not tonight." Pam will believe that he hasn't played fair and will resume criticizing him. He will believe that she hasn't really changed and will resume withdrawing.

The culprit in that scenario is poor communication. Pam and Paul didn't discuss their plans ahead of time and didn't let the other one know when they were trying to make positive changes. Pam should have said, "Paul, it looks like you could use some time to yourself. It's okay if you'd like to listen to some music." Then Paul would have realized she was making an effort. Or, Paul could have said, "I know you'd like me to talk more, so I thought I'd come out here in the kitchen to spend some time with you." Then Pam would have known he was making an effort.

The other reason why changes don't last is that people tend to drift back toward the status quo unless they stay mindful. This is a culture of quick fixes. Unfortunately, giving a lonely wife a little more attention or a harried husband a little more space can't be a seven-day fix. Additionally, couples often fail to appreciate each other's efforts at change. Often, they feel the other *should* be doing it that way, so they resist praising the effort. Or, they may be angry that it has taken so long to make changes that should have been made much sooner.

In my experience, if a frustrated woman halts her complaining and gives her man space, he doesn't automatically approach her more, talk more, or withdraw less. He tends to feel less pressure and likes the situation as it is. Eventually, the woman screams in frustration that her needs for intimacy are still not being met and the old cycle of criticize-withdraw resumes.

Why is that? On average, women are more concerned about the emotional connection in the relationship while men are concerned about preserving some separateness. Physiologically, it has been shown that men's heart rate and blood pressure rise to uncomfortable levels during conflict with their wives, and men try to withdraw from the discussion as a way to regulate their discomfort. Women respond with less physiological intensity and are able to withstand conflict better. In fact, Dr. Gottman's research suggests that once either partner's heart rate rises 10 percent above their preconflict level, physiology impedes good intentions. So a man with a resting heart rate of seventy-two beats per minute can add no more than seven extra beats before his ability to manage conflict deteriorates.

The need for intimacy versus the need for space also reflects a power difference between men and women. Men have more leverage. Men who need to isolate themselves (emotionally or physically) can do so on their own without a woman's help. But a woman's desire for intimacy cannot be met without cooperation from the man. He must be willing to move closer.

Unfortunately, once a woman stops pushing hard for intimacy, the man is more relaxed and content and not likely to automatically move in for closeness. The only time he does is when the woman has pulled too far away. That usually gets his attention. However, by that time the woman is not simply taking a timeout. She is fed up. She is emotionally drained and has begun questioning the value of the relationship. Only then do men sit up and take notice. But by that time, matters have deteriorated to the point of possible dissolution. When women feel "It's too little, too late," the situation is more than serious; it's usually over.

Unless a man (or the one who tends to withdraw from intimacy more often) is willing to make unilateral efforts to bridge the closeness gap, the woman in his life will be forever frustrated. She can learn to accept a little less intimacy than she desires if she believes she won't have to beg for every crumb. A man cannot use the fact that the woman is critical as his excuse to withdraw—because if she is less critical he will still withdraw. He must change in a direction that meets the woman's needs more often than not. He'll still have time for himself, and she'll be happy to let him have that time if she trusts there will be intimacy later on.

Deal with Conflict, and Don't Criticize

When discussing areas of conflict, men need to learn to hang in there and not withdraw prematurely from conversation. But women must learn to keep their criticisms in check. Accusing "You always . . . You never . . . Why can't you . . . You're such a . . ." and so forth will heighten her man's physiological discomfort and risk his shutting down. Below are four tips to reduce tension:

1. *Lower your heart rate.* This can be easily accomplished by "belly breathing." Place your hand on your stomach. As you inhale, your stomach should puff out. A calming breath should *not* cause your chest to puff out. This breathing pattern will trigger the part of your nervous system that calms you down.
2. *Remain seated during the conversation.* When one or both of you is standing, the odds are higher for more emotional responses or premature exits.
3. *State concerns, don't criticize.* Use the ABC method of talking. "When you say or do A, I think B, and feel C." ("When you tell me I don't care about you, I think about all the things I do for you, and I feel angry and misunderstood.") This method is more informative and less hostile than simply making blanket accusations.
4. *Praise each other during the conversation.* "I like the way you said that . . . You were nice not to interrupt . . . You seemed to listen well, I appreciate that."

Conflict-avoidance is not a problem if both members of the couple use that coping style and if the ratio of positive to negative interactions is at least five to one. Partners who avoid conflict usually learn to "agree to disagree" and they find it easier to tolerate their differences because most of their time together is pleasing and rewarding. But if time together is unfulfilling or if one partner does not like to avoid conflict, the above tips need to be followed.

The Dance of Defensiveness

A defensive person tries to deflect blame. He or she makes excuses for objectionable actions. We all do that from time to time. A defensive person sometimes feels attacked or accused when a partner was doing neither. Defensiveness becomes a problem in conversation because it gets in the way of listening and makes solutions harder to find. After all, if you're not to blame, someone else must be. But rarely is it that simple.

A defensive response can take many forms. Making excuses or denying the accusation is one way. Giving a snippy answer is another. Cross-complaining is a tactic whereby each partner accuses but neither one listens.

HE: *Do you always have to come home in a bad mood?*
SHE: *Maybe I wouldn't be in such a mood if you'd do the things I ask.*
HE: *Like what? It seems I'm responsible for everything around here and you get to relax.*
SHE: *Your voice is so annoying. Did I ever tell you that?*

Cross-complainers are lousy listeners and usually have a backpack full of resentments.

But some conversations can *appear* pleasant yet make one partner want to scream. When Millie asks her husband, Ben, what they should do this weekend, he usually responds, "Whatever you want." This drives her crazy. It bothers her because he is feigning interest when in reality he has little desire to do much of anything. This is a form of the pursue-withdraw pattern where Millie is in charge of the couple's recreation. He withdraws—subtly—by pretending to be enthusi-astic. But he offers no ideas and never initiates these kinds of conversations. When she complains, he blames her for making mountains out of molehills, and noth-ing gets resolved.

Relationship problems may begin because of one person, but they usually persist due to the misguided efforts of both people.

We don't like it when our mates get defensive, but the first thing to correct is our own way of talking. If we are criticizing or making accusations, our partner will inevitably get defensive. Most people would. The next thing is to analyze if our partner's defensive reaction is uncharacteristic. If so, cutting her some slack and asking if something's wrong (she could be having a bad day) is helpful. Still, even a perfectly worded complaint, laced with gentle tones, may not succeed. People sometimes speak defensively because that is their temperament and they simply want to halt the discussion, not because the other's concerns don't have merit.

If you have a concern that you want to raise but you think your mate will get defensive and the conversation will run amok, try this: "Honey, I want to ask you about something, but it's important that you listen first." Prefacing your concerns like that often helps. It gives them a chance to brace themselves for what they are sure is something they'd rather not hear. Once your partner has your complete attention, don't accuse. Say "It concerns me when . . ." Keep your voice at a conversational tone or slightly lower. Make the comments brief (you can add details later) and end them with words that have a soft touch. "I'd like us to find a way to change this so I don't feel so bad. How does that sound to you?"

If all your efforts seem futile, there is more going on than meets the eye. Not only does your partner not understand your concern, but there is something you may not fully understand about your partner. Probably it has to do with old hurts and misunderstandings that may even predate your relationship.

Some people get annoyed at advice to use softer words. They feel that they are being forced to tiptoe or walk on eggs. It feels unnatural and they resent having to choose their words carefully. The up-front, in-your-face, all-feelings-out-on-the-table kind of talk may seem open and honest, but it is like rubbing a scuffed knee with sandpaper. Such talk makes conversations more volatile, not less. Volatile couples can and do remain happily married, but the hostile conversations must be outweighed by many, many positive interactions.

You can't take potshots at your partner and expect the relationship to blossom. Name-calling and contemptuous cursing are especially corrosive. You can criticize once in a while, you can get defensive occasionally, but most of the time you have to sit and talk out your concerns in a way that shows respect and a team spirit.

13

are you listening to me?

Life is filled with hurts. Most are day-to-day stresses and letdowns, but they sometimes accumulate and bring us close to our breaking point. Tragedy and the pain of irretrievable loss are deeper, soul-aching hurts. But whatever problems we experience, our suffering is more piercing and makes us feel more hopeless when we do not feel that anyone is listening.

We want to be heard. We want to connect. We want to know that our problems—even our routine thoughts and feelings—can matter to somebody else. When those closest to us are poor listeners, the bumps and bruises of life seem more significant, more harsh, and less forgettable. And the tragedies are unbearable.

But when someone takes the time to really listen hard to what we have to say, we come away hopeful and less self-absorbed. Sometimes it is all we need to feel better and move on. Sometimes we need more.

∾ hear each other out with patience and love

The rules for making good conversation are as simple as the rules for making a soufflé. But give the ingredients to a chef and the soufflé will turn out much better than if it was prepared by someone with less skill. When couples try to communicate more effectively, the hardest thing to learn is how to listen. In fact, if you toss out all the rules for good communication except the rule for listening well, most conversations would soar to new heights, and couples who've drifted apart or who were caught in a tug-of-war would rediscover the closeness they once shared. Listening is not passive. Far from it. Done wrong, it comes off as a condescending pause, or a quiet sneer, as it would be when the so-called good listener sighs and says, "Are you finally finished? Can I get my turn now?" The words are reasonable, the tone may be quiet. But the attitude stabs.

It's a funny thing about very happy couples. They break many rules of communication yet get along fine. For example, everybody knows that interrupting your partner is a mistake. But one study revealed that happy couples interrupted each other 150 percent more often than unhappy couples. That was because happy couples viewed interruptions as signs that their mate was interested in the discussion. Unhappy couples construed interruptions as rude and disrespectful. The same is true with mind-reading. Most books will advise that mind-reading is ill advised. Couples mind-read when they presume to know what a mate is thinking or feeling without checking out their assumptions. "You're putting the kids to bed early because you just want to have sex with me" is an example. But research shows that happy couples do a lot of mind-reading. The difference is that unhappy couples are also showing negative emotions when they mind-read, whereas happy couples interpret mind-reading as a polite feeling probe. In the example above, a woman who is happy in her relationship may smile when she says, "You're putting the kids to bed early because you just want to have sex with me." And that will be followed immediately by smiling from him and a lot of playful fun. An unhappy woman will make the same comment with anger or cynicism in her voice. You can guess what will happen after that.

When Listeners Don't Hear Well

"You're not listening to me, Jack."

"I *am* listening, or at least I'm trying. But you're not making it easy. All you do is criticize and act like you're right and I'm wrong."

"Well, maybe I *am* right. But even if I'm not, you're not showing any interest in understanding my point of view. I just want you to listen. Is that too much to ask?"

"No. But evidently it's too much to ask you to stop talking to me like I'm the enemy. I'm only your husband, for God's sake."

Couples often talk like that. Each one wants to be listened to, but neither wants to be the first one to make it happen. When misunderstandings and resentments have accumulated, each partner feels more like a victim and digs in their heels. They each have the attitude that they will only listen *after* they have been listened to (if then). If you insist that your partner understand you before you understand him or her, you are acting from hurt and pride instead of extending love.

A good listener can increase the odds that the speaker won't have to chatter or whine or accuse. Speakers only do that when their past experiences showed them they were not being heard and not being cared about.

> *The truth is that while some people make it hard for others to listen to them—they chatter, they whine, they accuse, they yell, they complain, and they reject well-intended advice—the listener is still in the driver's seat.*

But why won't a listener listen well? Because he brings with him his temperament, his memories, his defensiveness, and fatigue. He may be preoccupied with other matters. His knee might be bothering him. Some people, men especially, listen to another's feelings and view them as problems to be solved, not as experiences to be understood. Often the speaker doesn't even understand her feelings yet, that's why she's talking about them and hoping someone is truly hearing what she's trying to say.

POOR LISTENERS

Following are the characteristics of poor listeners. You may recognize these traits in your partner or perhaps in yourself. Poor listeners:

- Are impatient.
- Spend too much time thinking about their response rather than listening to what's being said.
- Think they understand and rarely do.
- Are self-focused.
- Are emotionally reactive to what's being said. They can't empathize with the other person because they are too busy with their own feelings.

- Look for what's wrong or irrational about what's being said, instead of trying to convey that they understand. (A listener who says, "So it hurts you when I come home from work and ignore you. You feel like you don't matter," is showing he understands, even if he disagrees with her perspective.)
- Are afraid of what they might hear so they listen with their emotional guns cocked.
- Sometimes try to make others feel better with pat advice. They don't really want to understand the other person's pain. They want to tell them why they shouldn't be feeling that way. But if they truly understood, they'd know why the person feels that way.
- Take offense at the first sign of conflict. At that point they stop trying to understand.
- Don't think they are doing enough unless they offer reassurance or advice.
- Don't realize that if they do not listen better, someone else will replace them in the listening department. (And perhaps in other departments, too.)

How to Listen Without Lousing It Up

Imagine that your beloved is very upset (probably with you) and is complaining. Your job is to listen. But I mean *really listen* until you can put yourself in his shoes and try to experience what he is thinking and feeling. Doing that requires many things.

First, slow down. This is not a race. Understanding takes time. If you show your partner that you are willing to be patient and that he can speak without you trying to challenge him, he will slow down, too. And you'll each feel more relaxed.

If every listener tripled the amount of sincere listening and offered one-third of the advice, relationships would run more smoothly.

When speakers are running off at the mouth, it's often because they expect the gavel to slam down on their time. You have all the time in the world. Tell your partner that.

Second, interrupt every minute or so (yes, it's okay to interrupt if you do it for a good reason), but only to clarify your understanding of what's been said. If you let the speaker talk for minutes on end, there will be no way he will think you really got it all.

Your job is to make a quick, concise statement in your own words that reflects what the speaker was trying to tell you. Here are some examples:

"Let me just be sure I understand so far. You're saying that every time I go to my parents' home I ignore you and don't stand by you when my parents make critical comments. Is that right?"

"You're angry when I come home from work in a bad mood. Correct?"

"You're frustrated because it seems I give you mixed messages. Some days I like to hold your hand and other days I act like I want to be left alone. Is that what you are saying?"

"You want me to take more of an interest in our vacation plans. You feel overburdened that you are making all the arrangements."

If the speaker agrees with your assessment, let him continue. Only when he has felt completely understood is it time to respond with your viewpoint.

When listening, don't challenge your partner, don't make faces, roll your eyes, or groan. Don't jump in with comments such as, "You're wrong . . . That's not what happened . . . How could you say that? . . . I don't believe you're saying this . . . You're jumping to conclusions . . . You're being ridiculous . . . "

Remember, understanding your partner does not imply agreement. You want to understand how your mate is looking at things, not whether it is accurate.

Don't say "I understand." Even if you do understand, that comment is too shallow to have meaning. Too often it sounds like you're impatient and saying, "Yeah, yeah. Is it my turn yet?"

Helpful phrases while your mate is talking include: "Tell me more . . . That must have hurt . . . No wonder you're upset . . . Have you felt like this before? . . . Keep going, I want to try and understand . . . I can see why that bothered you . . . "

When you've slowed things down and are trying to communicate your understanding, the third thing you must do is put aside your own strong emotions. This is very difficult but very important. Otherwise, you are saying that *your* emotions and *your* point of view are more important than your mate's. Your partner won't like that. It is easier to put aside your emotions if you trust you will eventually be heard. Obviously, it takes time and practice before you can trust that will happen. But intense emotional responding will interfere with your dialogue and ensure that you may never be listened to the way you want.

It's okay (when it's your turn to speak) to comment on your inner emotional reactivity. "It was hard listening to you because you said things I thought were unfair. But I did my best to listen . . . I felt my stomach tighten and my heart race when you started calling me names. Please don't do that next time. It makes it harder for me to listen."

Sometimes you have strong emotional reactions when you are trying to listen because your partner pushed some buttons that were there long before she came into your life. Maybe your parents or your boss or your ex-wife were quick to blame you for things or failed to show their appreciation. If so, the next time your partner makes those mistakes you will react like you've been struck with a cattle prod. Better to say something along these lines:

YOU: *When you complain like that and I think you're being unfair, I get mad like I used to with my mother.*

HER: *But I'm not your mother. And besides, you do act in ways that are not easy to appreciate!*

YOU: *I'm sure I do. But what I need you to understand is that when you complain in a harsh way, it is harder for me to listen. I want to listen and I want to understand. I'm asking for your help with this.*

HER: *Your past is not my problem.*

YOU: *I'm working on overcoming it. I'm asking that you not make it more difficult. I know I frustrate you.*

In this example, the woman was particularly difficult. But it is possible to respond in ways that reduce conflict and tension instead of increasing it.

In happy relationships, partners learn how to de-escalate an argument. One of the best ways to do that is to listen attentively and not to challenge what you hear until you have commented on your understanding of (not necessarily agreement with) what was just said.

Typically, each partner becomes too emotionally reactive and the conversation spins out of control. But all it takes is one of you to respond patiently, such as in the above example, and things start to improve. Will the patient person be you?

～

If listening is hard for you, practice on people whom you are not so emotionally attached to. Let the guy at work talk about his brand-new car or his daughter's dance recital. Don't just stay quiet when listening. Ask brief questions that draw out the speaker and that show you are interested. Don't bring up your own kid's dance lessons or your car shopping stories. Say things such as, "You seem real happy you got such a good deal . . . You feel real proud of your daughter, I can tell . . . It annoys you how expensive cars have gotten ... You worried that your daughter might get nervous before her performance ... "

When you listen well—even if it looks like you are trying to listen well—you are doing more to promote well-being and happiness than you realize. And your relationships that matter will shine.

Once we start giving advice or fixing feelings, we have stopped trying to understand because we think we know all there is to know.

PART THREE
mistakes of the heart

14

I'll always love you . . . unless, of course, things change

"I'm not only in love with you," Jeff said to his fiancée, Carol. "I'm committed to you. I am completely devoted to you and always will be."

Carol smiled faintly. "I hear your words," she said. "And I believe that you believe them. But I've been married before and have heard those words before. What happens if love fades or you feel less attracted to me? Will you still remain committed?"

Carol's question was a good one. She was tapping into one of the key mistakes of the heart that couples in love (especially young couples) make: defining commitment according to the level of happiness that exists in the relationship. ("Of course I'm committed to you. I *love* you!") The truth is less romantic but more noble and mature: Commitment is a decision, not a feeling. It may be fed by emotions of love and desire, but it is anchored in place by choice and moral integrity. Emotions shift. Commitment must be sturdier. It is not difficult to commit to someone you love. It is harder but critically important to remain committed when adversity strikes or passion withers. Otherwise, you are not devoted to the other person. You are devoted only to the feeling of being in love.

❧ commit fully, not halfheartedly

Hot romance is exhilarating. Remember? The passion and excitement of a new relationship helps to push it along to the next phase: commitment. If the "c" word sounds too sterile, try "devotion." There is no fullness of love—whatever your hormones tell you—when there is no commitment, no deep devotion.

Lack of commitment is "I love you" with an asterisk.

Relationships without commitment may be powerfully intoxicating (the fall-in-love phase), or they may be practical (living together to save money), but they lack the depth and richness that committed, devotional love possesses. Your partner may be thoughtful, considerate, and a fantastic lover, and your pillow talks may be intimate and revealing. But lack of commitment means he or she wants the option to leave on a moment's notice.

An uncommitted partner may be a friend or companion. But is that all you want? Think of your best friend. If he or she moves across the country, are you likely to follow? Probably not. You may write to each other, call, and visit, but you have not fully committed your life to that person. If you want to spend your life with a person and perhaps raise children together, commitment (the decision, not the feeling) is essential.

Linking commitment to passion is a mistake of the heart that young couples in particular make. Twenty percent of all divorces occur within the first two years of marriage. Forty percent occur within the first four years. Compared to longer-married couples, young couples don't wait until they are miserable before they divorce. Their tolerance for unhappiness is lower. Thus, it requires higher levels of marital satisfaction for them to remain married. This means that they commit to each other as long as they feel in love. When the feeling fades, so does the commitment. However, commitment is meaningless if it is abandoned when the relationship is going through hard times.

Why are younger couples less committed? There are many reasons. The odds are high that at least one partner was raised in a divorced family. Statistics show that children of divorced parents have a higher rate of divorce themselves, are less trusting of mates, and are less adept at resolving conflicts. Also, when people are young there are still many attractive alternatives to their current partner, and divorce is not the social stigma it once was. Additionally, in the search for true happiness, many people seek pleasure. What they fail to grasp is that pleasure is always fleeting and that true joy comes from mutual and deep devotion through committed love. That type of true love is sacrificial, however. It means giving something up once in a while. Some people resent having to make any sacrifices.

Three Types of Commitment

When a couple says they are committed, what they often mean is this: "I'm devoted to you *because* I love you." This type of commitment is attraction-based and hinges upon the feelings of happiness being sustained. It doesn't require getting married as proof of one's commitment. It is a form of commitment that is powerful yet one-dimensional.

A more profound commitment is moral-based. It includes the attraction-based commitment but takes it a meaningful leap forward. It is a commitment to the marriage vows and to your partner's human dignity and spiritual growth. It means a willingness to remain devoted to the other person despite hardship, fluctuations in passion, and more appealing alternatives. It contains the belief that marriage as an institution is worth preserving.

A third type is empty commitment. That happens when people remain in a relationship purely out of dire necessity, entrapment, or obligation. Usually these couples cannot afford to separate, or one partner is too dependent upon the other. Sometimes a person is unwilling to divorce for religious reasons but is not committed to his or her spouse in any other way. Love is absent in these cases.

The old axiom is true: A solid relationship is like a well-built house. The walls and roof remain standing only if the foundation is strong. It is a mistake of the heart to make the foundation a commitment based on attraction, happiness, or passion. The strongest foundation in a relationship is a moral-based commitment. Why? Because the feelings of being in love shift. We may *know* we love our partner, but we don't always *feel* it. Also, when commitment is primarily attraction-based, partners don't completely trust each other. There remains a nagging doubt that their love will stand the tests of time or adversity. That diminished trust will reveal itself in many ways that further undermine the strength of the relationship: It can create heightened neediness or cause one to pull back a bit; it can incite suspiciousness; it can cause you to look to other potential partners as a "backup."

We must be stronger than our feelings. And when problems arise, as they do in most people's lives, anger or hurt can whittle away our love and caring much faster when there is no full commitment.

Imagine that you are committed to becoming a champion swimmer or a lead violinist in a symphony. You not only love to play music or swim, you value the occupation and believe it is a wonderful and noble goal. Most people fail at goals because they are not willing to pay the price for success. Loving the sport or the music isn't enough. What sacrifices will you make? If you injure your arm will you somehow persevere? When you get occasionally bored will you hang in there? If you get frustrated by others, if they criticize you, take advantage of you, or fail to offer encouragement when needed, will you still do what you must do to succeed?

You may commit yourself to another person because you love him and the relationship is working, but then you must keep your commitment— despite fluctuations in desire and changes in your life—to keep that relationship working.

Loving the sport or the music is not sufficient if you don't commit yourself to the ongoing, ever-changing process. But commitment without the love will be empty and unsatisfying. You need both.

Commit to Choose, Then Choose to Commit

Every couple needs a certain amount of closeness and a certain amount of separateness. But when you are not fully committed, you will never fully give yourself to the relationship. You will add distance at the expense of closeness. You will hold back just enough love or intimacy or self-sacrifice to keep you from feeling vulnerable or out of control. But since your relationship does not exist in a vacuum, your partner will react to those withholding ways. Maybe she'll pursue you more as she gets more insecure about your love and devotion. That will threaten your need for distance and you'll pull back farther. Or maybe she'll get angry. Either way, the relationship will become tenser and you will have even more reason to resist committing to it.

If your partner is not fully committed and you remain in the relationship, you will go on a roller-coaster ride. Some days you'll move cautiously, not wanting to upset things. Other days you'll lunge closer, needing a strong sign that you are still loved and wanted. Your instincts tell you that love without commitment is pleasurable at times, but basically hollow. It can lead you to despair.

Since commitment is ultimately a decision, you must first *commit yourself to choosing*. It is the choice to be a player, not an observer; active, not reactive. You must choose to do the kinds of things that people in truly committed relationships do:

- Agree that marriage is your ultimate goal
- Remain sexually faithful
- Stay devoted to one another's dreams; help to fulfill them
- Show caring on a regular basis
- Hold up your end of the bargain
- Overlook the other's shortcomings
- Try to change some of your own shortcomings
- Never idly threaten separation or divorce
- Never purposely make your partner insecure

Once you commit to choosing, you must *choose to commit* to the choices you've made. Don't retreat at the first sign of difficulty. Don't say one thing and do another.

Some people claim they are committed. They claim they would never leave their partner. But they do very little to make the relationship fulfilling. If you know you cannot devote yourself to the other person, or if your partner is not devoted to you, you must honestly reevaluate the reasons for staying together.

Marge and Pete were married for seven years when she was diagnosed with a degenerative neurological disorder. While this disease can be slow in its progression, Marge's case was severe. Both active athletes, Marge was confined to her home most days. Vacations, even short weekend outings, were canceled and never could be planned, as Marge's condition often took sudden turns for the worse. Marge was unable to continue working. Their income dropped and they struggled to make the payments on their house. Their dream of having children had to be put aside.

I often spoke alone with Pete. Trying to be strong for his wife, he hesitated to discuss his fears with her. With tears in his eyes he'd speak glowingly of Marge's valiant efforts to persevere and fight her illness; of how he'd lift her and carry her from room to room on days her legs gave way; of how scared he was of one day losing her. He was exhausted physically and emotionally but never wavered in his commitment to Marge.

And Marge, while frightened of her debilitating condition, seemed to come alive when she spoke of her devotion to Pete. They were soul mates, unable to be torn apart by anything life threw at them.

Doug and Barbara had a different problem. After a nine-month separation where Doug had begun dating and then living with another woman, he returned home. Barbara knew he still had feelings for the other woman. Barbara believed that he came back because he didn't want a divorce, not because he loved her. In fact, she believed he loved the other woman more. It was understandable that Barbara would be dissatisfied, yet she regarded his commitment to her as meaningless because it was not accompanied by great love. In fact, Doug was trying to turn his life around and keep the vows he had once made to her. He made a *decision* to try and work out his marriage, hoping it would eventually resurrect his passion for her. The *decision* aspect of commitment is crucial at times when the *emotional* bond is diminished. These two factors—emotion and decision—are two pillars that work together to keep a relationship alive.

Devotion Flows from Determination

Determination involves two qualities: persistence and purpose. Persistence is the legwork, the plodding forward when you're tired or weak or uncertain. It is the *how*. Purpose is the *why*. Persistence is your arms and legs and hands and feet. Purpose is your heart and soul.

In your relationship, it can be hard to learn to communicate more effectively, to give up something you'd like, to forgive, or to be patient with a partner. But you will persist in your efforts to make your relationship a success if you have a strong, underlying purpose.

Your commitment will be stronger when you unite purpose and persistence. When your commitment is sagging, it is a good idea to remind yourself of the positive purpose for keeping the relationship afloat. Without it, you will grow weary and depressed.

Positive purpose provides meaning to your adversity. And the meaning you give it changes the level of pain and suffering. (If you suffered a severe injury rescuing your child, your pain would mean something different to you than if you suffered the same injury in a careless accident.) Meaning makes pain tolerable and allows you to persevere. It can change tragedy into a triumph of love. Just ask Marge and Pete.

Commitment Strategies

Commitment is not a noose around your neck. Some relationships should end. If your partner repeatedly acts in ways that show cruelty or indifference, then he has proven his lack of commitment to you and to the relationship.

But commitment is also harder to sustain when you have nagging doubts or recurring problems that have whittled down your hope and love. Commitment may then be halfhearted. Maybe you try to improve the relationship but don't have the energy to keep trying. Maybe you don't want to leave, but you're not always happy about staying, either. Keep these tips in mind:

- Your behavior is not a simple by-product of your attitude. ("I show love because I feel love.") How you act also affects your attitude. ("If I show less love, I will feel less love.") Choose to act more committed to your mate despite doubts. Ask yourself: *What would I be doing and saying if I was more committed?* Then do and say some of those things. You are not being phony. You are trying to resurrect an attitude that hopefully still exists, though it is weakened.

- Shake off the cobwebs and try to see your partner's qualities that made you fall in love in the first place. Plan several dates in the near future where you can focus on those qualities. Dissatisfied partners overemphasize their mate's flaws and underemphasize their positive traits.

- Be alert for "pursuer-distancer" patterns in your relationship. Often, one partner is trying to make improvements while the other is nonresponsive. When the first partner backs away in frustration, the second partner eventually gets nervous and finally approaches, but the first partner is now nonresponsive. This pattern maintains the status quo and gives each partner the *false perception* that they are committed and cooperative, while their partner is not. The key is to recognize that each of you wants things to improve but each of you is also skittish. Don't let the other person be your excuse to back away. Each must move forward at the same time.

- Never make idle threats about separation or divorce. Once that happens, everything you say or do will be analyzed under the microscope of skepticism or mistrust.

- If your lover is married to someone else but promises he'll get a divorce and commit himself to you, be extremely wary. Only in about 10 percent of cases does a couple in an extramarital affair end up married. The sad but painful truth is this: Most of the passion of an affair is stoked by the drama of secrecy. It is also more desirous because it is being compared to one partner's unhappy marriage. Once that marriage ends, the affair relationship has to stand on its own. Rarely does it have the legs to do so.

- Don't be too shy to demonstrate publicly that your mate is your chosen comrade. Go out of your way to kiss or hug hello even if others are watching. Hold hands more often. Don't ignore him or her in conversations with others. Show observers that you love and respect one another.

If your love is a fire, commitment is the kindling. Without it, the warmth of your passion cannot be sustained.

15

can't you just get over it?

Richard should have been humble. He should have been begging for mercy. Instead he was growing defiant and resentful. His live-in mate for the past three years—Sharon, the woman to whom he promised his devotion—had finally stopped yelling at him for the moment. He hadn't interrupted, he knew better than that, but he'd also tuned her out. It had been four months since she discovered his secret affair and three months and three weeks since he ended it. Richard wanted his relationship with Sharon to continue. The problem was that Sharon had been on an emotional roller coaster since his affair was revealed. Once or twice they even made love with a passion they hadn't experienced before. But most days she wanted nothing to do with him sexually, and little to do with him otherwise. She just berated him or asked him questions over and over like a prosecuting attorney hell-bent on the death penalty. On better days she acted polite but distant, like she would to an unwelcome guest. He almost preferred the yelling. He was miserable and fed up. His first mistake, obviously, was having an affair. But his second mistake, the one that most unfaithful partners make when trying to repair the broken relationship, was his attitude that Sharon "should be over it by now."

Unfaithful partners who want their relationship to move forward are frequently their own worst enemy. Apologetic and ashamed at first (if they are not, the relationship is in serious trouble), they grow weary of their mate's anger and over time (usually within three or four months) throw down the gauntlet. They want the affair to be in the past and they blame their faithful partner for prolonging the agony. It is a mistake of the heart that makes their situation worse.

∾ ask for forgiveness through humility and true remorse

Is cheating common? Are the odds high that in a marriage there will eventually be infidelity? The answers may surprise you.

Many surveys show a high incidence of infidelity, but these are not scientifically conducted. In fact, the first scientific survey (by the Gallup organization) using population sampling techniques did not occur until 1989 and was funded by *Psychology Today* magazine. It showed affairs occurred in 10 percent of all marriages. It also showed that in any given year, 96 percent of married partners remain faithful. The second scientific survey was conducted by the University of Chicago in 1994. It revealed that over 90 percent of women and over 75 percent of men are faithful over the entire course of their marriage. And when you consider that many affairs are what author Carol Rhodes calls "bridge affairs"—a way to get out of a marriage that's bound to end anyway—then it becomes clear that monogamy is a highly respected practice within intact marriages. In fact, three-quarters of adulterers would remarry their spouse if given the chance. So Richard's desire to stay with Sharon despite his affair is not unusual or surprising.

Popular print and television media promote the bias that sexual unfaithfulness occurs in most marriages eventually. The truth is far different.

Infidelity rates are higher for unmarried cohabiting couples. But the crucial attitude was revealed by answering the question: Would you have an affair if you knew you could get away with it? People who answered yes were more likely to be unfaithful, whether they were married or just living together. But those who are disposed to cheat are also more likely to cohabit.

What happens when the couple mishandles the reconciliation after infidelity? Whether or not the couple is married, predictable stages follow:

1. *Rehash/Guilt:* The offender (say, the husband) guiltily listens to his wife as she frequently points out the harm he has caused. He hates being reminded of it, but he knows he deserves it.

2. *Quicksand:* He grows weary of his past actions being thrown in his face. By now, his wife has asked the same questions repeatedly and she may be unsure he has told her the complete truth. He fears that they will never climb out of this quicksand.

3. *Battle Stations:* He resents the inquisition and the fact that her bringing up the past ruins their good times. He tells her so. She shoots back that he obviously has no idea of the pain he has put her through. (This is the stage where Richard and Sharon find themselves.)

4. *Resistance/Surrender:* In order to put an end to the long trial, he becomes hostile and uncooperative. He refuses to answer questions he has answered many times already. She accuses him of hiding something. Often, the "other woman" has reentered the scene in a minor but toxic way—perhaps he bumped into her at work, or she phoned him just to see how he was doing, or they saw her at a restaurant. His wife wants to know why he even looked at or spoke to the woman. He gets defensive and she accuses him of caring more about the other woman's feelings than hers. He says she's being ridiculous. She's more convinced he hasn't the faintest idea of what he has put her through. At this point, it is not the sexual aspect of his affair that hurts her the most, but rather his deceit and his current inability to realize the pain she still suffers.

5. *Exhaustion/Relief:* It is months later and the couple is emotionally exhausted. They either learn to get along despite underlying anger, or they consider splitting up. If they're lucky, they realize the mistakes they've made during the previous four stages and take steps to correct them.

Healing Wounds

The more affairs a person has, the more likely the person will continue having them. He or she may be someone with a diminished capacity for empathy (and therefore love) or someone who is addicted to sex. But many people who have affairs are weak or lonely, not bad or addicted people. Often, affairs happen without a premeditated intent. They begin as friendships or as chat room companionship, and matters get out of hand. In these cases, the one having the affair isn't that happy in the marriage, but neither is he doing all he can to make the marriage work. Many affairs are "emotional affairs" that do not involve sex (yet) but do involve intense emotional intimacy. Usually such people are confidants and view one another as exceptional listeners with a deep capacity for caring.

There are many reasons people offer for having affairs, but none of them is good enough for the offended spouse. The bottom line is that having an affair is a lousy thing to do to a partner, especially if you might want your marriage to continue.

The process of healing from an affair takes much time. In the best cases, there will be significant improvement over the course of a year, but the offended party still keenly feels flashes of anger and deep pain. Often, a year isn't long enough. That's because the way in which the couple tried to get past the affair made their situation worse.

Following are the most common mistakes made by the guilty person in the effort to reconcile.

MISTAKE: He says he understands the pain his partner is going through, but he really does not. That is not because he doesn't care. It is because he feels guilt and pain while watching his loved one suffer. After a while he can't tolerate that guilt. But his mistake is blaming his wife for her inability to let the past go.

SOLUTION: Suffer your guilt. Realize that every day your partner suffers more than you. She is haunted by your affair, grieved by your breaking of vows, and frightened she may never be able to trust you again. She needs your steadfast resolve to hang in there and not condemn her for her ongoing mistrust and anger. When she says she cannot trust you, what she might want to hear is something like, "I know, I don't blame you for that. I know that I am trustworthy now and will never hurt you again. But I also know it will take you a long time to believe that. I am so grateful you are hanging in there with me."

MISTAKE: At some point he feels that he has paid his dues. That only reveals to his spouse just how little he really understands the pain he has caused.

SOLUTION: Better to say that you are scared or worried that she will never trust you again. That expresses your concern without further offending her.

MISTAKE: He stops answering questions he has answered many times before. He resents being put on trial day after day.

SOLUTION: Keep answering them with patience. She's asking them not to torture you, but because she is tortured by the affair and cannot let go just yet. Her mind is replaying everything because a part of her hasn't let it sink in completely. Give her more time.

MISTAKE: He won't answer blunt and embarrassing questions. He says it would only make his wife feel worse. (Some spouses don't want to know all the details of the affair. However, most usually are haunted by their imagination and need to know details that are sexually graphic. They hate hearing the answers but feel their sanity will crumble if they don't hear them.)

SOLUTION: If she asks for the details, provide them. Do so with great gentleness and sorrow, neither hedging nor displaying a "There, are you satisfied?" attitude.

MISTAKE: He stops trying to reassure his spouse of his trustworthiness. He grows tired of "checking in" as it makes him feel like a child. He forgets to call when he'll be late.

SOLUTION: You won't have to prove your trustworthiness forever. But you will have to do so for longer than you think. In many ways your partner has been traumatized; her world is upside down. Being careless about informing her where you are going or how long you will be triggers frightening memories.

MISTAKE: He gets angry when a nice weekend together is marred by his wife's fluctuating moods. Often the bad mood is triggered by something such as a TV show about an affair, or a drive by a restaurant she knew he took his lover to.

SOLUTION: State you understand. Don't sulk or get angry. Mention how you know it must be awful for her. She'll recover faster if you show compassion, not insensitivity.

It is usually a very good idea for the couple to schedule their discussions about the affair instead of letting them occur randomly. The woman (or the offended party) needs to know that her anger and worries can be vented and that her mate will cooperate in the conversation rather than stonewall. The man (or the guilty party) needs to know that certain times will be free from these discussions so that a more normal lifestyle can be resumed. If the couple schedules discussions ahead of time (say, twice a week for an hour at specified times), both parties are more likely to get their needs met. But the wife must not ask questions or make jabs at unspecified times, and the husband must cooperate fully in answering her questions during the scheduled hour.

The offended party usually makes mistakes in this reconciliation process, too. Initially, she is allowed much room to vent. But if she takes potshots at her mate (however justified), it corrodes the process. At first she asks a multitude of questions, but eventually asks questions that have no good answer. Asking the simple question "Why did you cheat on me?" has no answer she will find acceptable. Yet she repeats it.

Wanting her mate to "check in" is usually necessary. But over time she must be willing to take chances. Trust means having faith when you don't know for sure. Unless she gives him freedom to move around, she'll never develop faith.

Eventually, she must look at her own flaws. It is unreasonable to say that any of her flaws "caused" her husband to have the affair. However, if the relationship was far from perfect, the wife should try to identify her own mistakes in the relationship in order to help herself trust him. Improving those personal areas can give her a hopeful sense that the marriage can indeed change for the better. It places some of the focus on herself, where she has control, instead of on him, where she has less control.

LOGGING ON FOR FUN AND FANTASY:
A RISK NOT WORTH TAKING

Not surprisingly, sex is the number one Internet search topic. Two-thirds of browsers are men. The numbers are hard to come by, but therapists everywhere are seeing a huge increase in online "affairs" that can ruin a relationship just as much as the old-fashioned affair can. Chat room affairs seem innocent at first. There is no touching, no dating, no "real" cheating—except that an intimacy sometimes develops. For some, it is meant as a game that results in talking dirty and masturbation. For others, a serious relationship evolves. Either way, it can be a threat to the real-life relationship at home. Online lovers get into private chat rooms and converse for hours, often late at night, which adds to the romantic feel. They lie to their real-life partners about what they are doing and how often. They may pretend that it is not really cheating, but it is. (A good rule to follow: If you aren't sure whether what you are doing constitutes cheating, ask your mate.) Bypassing the chat rooms and heading straight for the sex shows on the Web can also be destructive. While many men claim such an interest is normal, the wide variety of pornography and instant access that the Internet provides make this more risky than browsing through an adult magazine. The following are clues that the situation is very serious:

- You are sneaking onto the site.
- You have made up a chat room name or persona.

- You masturbate while online.
- You are asked to stop but do not.
- You can't wait to get online.

If you want your mate to trust you and if you want to honor your mate, click on something safe.

If you have had an affair but want to salvage your relationship, genuine remorse is essential. That means you'll think more about how you hurt your partner than how you have been hurt. It means you'll want to make amends. It means you will give your mate much time to heal, and understand when she is having a hard time doing so. It means looking inward to discover your weaknesses and try to change them. If you handle it right, you and your mate can recover from an affair. It is well worth the effort.

16
I should have known better

The simplest and best way to manage problems in a relationship is to prevent them from happening in the first place. But this requires partners to see the early warning signs. Unfortunately, when a couple is falling in love, their emotions take charge and their intuition and common sense are brushed aside. It is a mistake of the heart that some couples will pay for dearly months and years later.

Relationship conflicts often occur in three stages. At stage one, the problems are sensed but easily dismissed. A perceptive mate might ask, "Is something wrong?" but not push it if he is told, "No, nothing is wrong." When Adam and Dena had been dating for a few months, Dena needed to buy a new car. Adam went along to offer his opinion, but Dena had a pretty clear idea of what she wanted. When she was making a deal with the salesperson, Adam interrupted and told her, "You don't really want this car. It's too expensive. You can save money and do just as well with a different model." He then stood up, took Dena's hand, and walked her outside.

Dena was not amused. She thought Adam had crossed a line. He patiently listened and then told her that she would realize later on that he was right. "I'm only looking out for your best interest," he said.

Dena ignored this warning sign. Adam was treating her like a child, but she convinced herself that her anger was an overreaction. When she moved in with Adam six months later, his tendency to want to take control of situations became more obvious. Everything had to be his way. If she complained, he accused her of being difficult and inflexible. Dena finally left him, but she had to scramble to find a new apartment. She kicked herself for giving up her old place to be with a jerk like Adam.

At stage two, the problems are aboveboard. The couple has the opportunity to discuss their differences and try to arrive at a solution that meets one another's needs. But at this stage, the couple can also wander down a rocky path. They may get into a battle of wills. One may give in but over time become bitter or depressed. Or, one may apply a "solution" that was never discussed and may be totally inappropriate, and then get upset at the partner when the solution doesn't work. For example, Phil was perturbed that Holly's extra work assignments caused her to go to bed late. When she finally joined him in bed, he acted cold and sulked. It was his way of expressing anger indirectly, and it was his attempt at a solution. (He figured Holly would realize she was wrong and be apologetic. Boy, was he wrong.) Holly hated that side of Phil. He'd never complain about something until it was too late and then he'd act like a victim.

A battle of wills is often an unwillingness to see one's own role in a problem.

So her solution was to leave the bed and go to the couch "to read." That would teach him a lesson, she thought. She imagined it would prompt him to come crawling to her eventually, begging for forgiveness. She was wrong, too. After a month they rarely went to bed at the same time anymore. When they did, the tension was thick. Neither one wanted to be conciliatory. The story has a happy ending, but Phil and Holly had to go through a lot of unnecessary pain before they worked things out.

At stage three, the couple has grown far apart. Each one is bitter and believes that the other one is more to blame. Neither wants to extend an olive branch because they feel they are owed. Each is accusatory, defensive, contemptuous, and avoiding of the other. The relationship is so unsatisfying that each partner devotes more energy to other areas (the kids, hobbies, work, etc.), and they grow further apart. When they finally decide to improve the situation, they each have a low tolerance for any setbacks and are quick to say "Why bother?"

You don't want to get to stage three. It is extremely difficult to make the relationship work from that stage. By the time you arrive there you have experienced too much anger and heartache. But chances are that the early warning signs were all around you. Had you heeded them, you would have been spared emotional anguish. But will you allow your brain, not your heart, to do your thinking for you?

∾ address (don't suppress) the early warning signs

People ignore the early signs because of varying degrees of insecurity and immature psychological adjustment. Unfortunately, "like attracts like." A mature, secure adult will not be attracted to someone too far from his level of maturity. An initial (perhaps sexual) attraction may exist, but the well-adjusted person will not pursue the relationship further. (For example, a mature person in his late twenties would no longer be romantically attracted to a senior in high school. The senior would be too immature.) So a somewhat insecure adult with a history of a some bad relationships or bad choices (dating a verbally abusive man, for example) is likely to attract someone who is similarly insecure (though their areas of insecurity may be different). Just as a senior in high school may not recognize the immaturity of a classmate (though she will recognize the immaturity of, say, a ninth grader), a decent but somewhat insecure thirty-year-old may not see the flaws in her new partner that are obvious to others.

One middle-aged woman whose miserable marriage was about to end, fell in love with a man who had fathered three children by three different women (all out of wedlock). She viewed him as troubled but misunderstood. He moved in with her and within six months her life was "a living hell." Finally, he left her and moved in with another woman. She was shell-shocked at first but soon realized she was better off.

Warning Signs

Even a relationship with everything going against it can flourish. But that usually doesn't happen. When a couple ignores the following warning signs, their relationship will probably deteriorate over time and end in disaster.

GET OUT NOW

If any of these signs are present early on in your relationship, your best bet is to walk away before you get deeper into it. Get out now if your partner:

- *Is still married to someone else.* You never should want to be the person who helps break up a marriage. (Chances are good that once the marriage is over, *you'll* be history.) Unless a person takes time *between* relationships to sort out what went wrong, odds are the same mistakes will be repeated in the next relationship. If your new partner has been separated *and* a divorce is imminent, he or she may be ready to start a new relationship. But proceed cautiously.

- *Gets into trouble with the law.*

- *Has a history of irresponsible and reckless behavior.* He gets fired a lot; quits jobs when he has bills to pay but doesn't seem to care; is behind in child-support payments; has had children out of wedlock; has gotten into serious debt due to flagrant mismanagement of funds.

- *Is actively alcoholic (or addicted to drugs, sex, or gambling).* Such a person is not capable of giving in an emotionally healthy way, however sorry you feel for him. Reconsider when he's been sober for at least a year.

- *Has different goals and values than you in key areas.* He wants children, but you don't; he doesn't want to get married, but you do; religion is very important to him but not important to you; she likes to spend money on extravagant items, but you are budget conscious; and so on. Disagreement on values is a predictor of divorce.

- *Thinks she always knows better than you and wants to run your life.*

- *Thinks you always know better than she does and wants you to run her life.* Some find this appealing initially. They like being needed and in charge. Eventually, their partner matures and resents being treated like a child. Such independent thinking will become a threat to the established relationship.

- *Is physically abusive.*

- *Is verbally abusive (name-calling, put-downs, blaming).* Calling someone a bitch or a bastard isn't necessarily abusive. But do other actions show you that he or she has contempt for you? Recurrent comments such as "What did I ever see in you? . . . You'll never be the man [woman] I want . . . You disgust me . . . No one ever got me this angry . . . " are red flags.

PROCEED WITH CAUTION

Some signs are more easily dismissed but should not be. They may not be as fatal as other signs, but they deserve your attention. Proceed slowly and cautiously if your partner:

- *Is emotionally cut off from his family of origin.* There may be good reason for putting distance between oneself and one's parents. However, the more cut off a person is, the greater the likelihood that you will pay the price for the sins of the parents. Your mate will be oversensitive to issues that originated in childhood and will be quick to feel rejected, abandoned, mistreated, or unappreciated by you. Emotional cutoffs tend to repeat during the next generation (that means your kids). If your mate has issues with his folks, a more mature response for him would be to keep in periodic (safe) contact with them, wish them well, and be open to a fuller reconciliation with them.
- *Is too dependent (emotionally or financially) on his family of origin.* A close family is terrific and a good sign. But if your mate puts family first and you last or seems to have lost a sense of independence and can't make a move without family approval, trouble may be on the horizon.
- *Is disliked by your family and friends.* Friends and family know you better than you think. If you trust their opinion and they have concerns, take them very seriously.
- *Has a significantly different background from you.* Diversity can be fine. But research shows that divorces are less likely if you and your partner have similar IQs, educational backgrounds, cultural experiences, or religious beliefs. Differences won't necessarily make a difference, but odds are they will become an issue.
- *Has broken up from an important relationship within six months of dating you.*
- *Cannot accept responsibility for any past relationship failures or current difficulties.*
- *Tends to be coercive.* If he keeps at you to do things you don't want to do, if he keeps trying to change you in ways you aren't comfortable changing, rethink this relationship.
- *Cannot accept you pretty much the way you are.* You do have flaws and some should be changed. However, you do not want to be in a relationship

where your mate is always after you to be different in some fundamental way (more ambitious, more sociable, less temperamental, less emotional, and so forth). Bad habits (smoking, sloppiness) can be modified. Character traits are likely to last.

- *Won't come to your defense if his parents or family unfairly criticizes you.* This is particularly important if you are engaged or recently married. By that time, your mate should be loyal to you. Even if his parents have a justifiable point to make against you, he should stand by you and at least tell his parents to keep their viewpoints to themselves. If his parents are clearly unfair, he should defend you. If he says, "That's the way my parents are. Let's not make a scene," then you are being asked to pay a price for his unassertiveness. (You are also being set up. He may suppress his anger at his parents but allow you to get angry at them instead.) If you choose to limit your contact with his parents, do not expect him to follow suit. He has a right to maintain his connection with them.

What Is Your Attachment Style?

A final clue to future relationship problems has to do with something called "attachment style." This refers to your sensitivity to intimacy and distance within a relationship. Often, one's attachment style can be traced to basic temperament, early life experiences, and how secure you felt growing up. For example, if a child is mistreated or rejected by a parent, the child will become insecure. There are basically three romantic attachment styles:

1. *Secure.* A secure person does not get too anxious when someone gets close, neither does she worry about being abandoned. She allows herself to be somewhat dependent on her partner, but knows he depends on her, too.
2. *Anxious.* These persons tend to smother a partner. They worry about being rejected or abandoned and only feel comfortable when they feel very close. Overdone, they tend to push people away, which makes them more anxious and more likely to seek greater closeness.
3. *Avoidant.* This person gets uneasy when too close. He prefers greater distance to closeness. He doesn't trust easily and often feels that his partner wants more closeness than he feels comfortable providing.

According to recent studies, about 55 percent of people form secure attachments, 20 percent form anxious attachments, and 25 percent form avoidant attachments. Interestingly, an avoidant partner often connects with an anxious partner, thereby making each one more tense and uneasy. One pushes for closeness while the other pulls away to get space. That is not an accident. The avoidant person pulls away, yet *he does want closeness.* So he hooks up with a woman who pushes for closeness. That way he knows he can have closeness whenever he wants, but he doesn't have to take responsibility for making it happen. The opposite is true for the anxious woman. She wants to be able to be more emotionally independent and to be able to trust, so she hooks up with a man who will pull away from her. She doesn't want to take responsibility for the independent times. If they get into a tug-of-war, the anxious person will only be aware of rejection and will therefore become more anxious, and the avoidant person will only be aware of being smothered, so he will pull back more. Each will act in more extreme ways and blame the other, without realizing that they are caught in a vicious cycle.

Your future, your mate's future, and your children's future are too important to take unnecessary risks. Warning signs should be examined and addressed. Anything less and you are allowing luck to be the controlling force.

17

just change these few things for me

People who jump into relationships and ignore warning signs of potential disaster are accepting things they should try to change (see chapter 16). But many people pick away like crows at their partners by insisting on changes that are unlikely to happen. Not only is it a waste of energy, but such coercive efforts build ill will. If you dislike a trait of your partner's, you will get even more annoyed if your efforts to get him to change yield no results. Then you'll view him as stubborn or inflexible or selfish. Since you also view your desire for him to change as reasonable ("He *should* be neater."), you will be reluctant to rethink your position ("Gee, maybe I'm expecting him to be too much like me."). If the battle of wills continues, then for you to "win" he must change. If you accept him the way he is, it feels like you lose. (A partner may refuse to change because he resents your inability to accept him. Ironically, if you did accept some of his flaws, he might actually change them.) All couples are incompatible in some areas. When there is conflict or differences of opinion, you have only two choices: make changes or accept matters as they are.

A relationship in which changes aren't being made won't be satisfying, but a relationship without acceptance won't last. Many of us would like our partners to change while we think that they should accept us. It's hard for us to admit we're not thoroughly lovable, either, just the way we are.

❧ honor by accepting

Hal wanted to make love four or five times a week. His wife Ginny was content with having sex about once a week or (preferably) less. This difference became harder for them to tolerate because each one believed the other was unreasonable. *Why couldn't Ginny just go along with having sex more often?* Hal thought. He didn't buy her argument that she was busy and tired because he noticed she seemed to spend extra hours on the phone during the week with her friends. Didn't she have time for him? Ginny thought that sex was all Hal ever thought about. Maybe if he'd clean up around the house more and walk the dog he absolutely had to own, she'd have more time for him.

"If you loved me," Ginny said, "you'd back down and respect my wishes without pressuring me."

"Well, if you loved me," Hal shot back, "you'd respect my wishes and have sex more often. You know you could make the time. You're just choosing not to."

While mismatched sexual desire is not unusual among couples, the difference between Hal's and Ginny's desire was striking. Should one of them simply accept the situation and give in to their partner's wishes? Probably not. They may indeed have different sex drives, but their resentment has inflamed the situation. Each feels mistreated. If both could be more sympathetic and reassuring to the other, their differences in sex drive would still exist but to a lesser extent. For example, if Hal would say, "It's okay if we don't have sex. But I'd still like to hold you in bed," or if Ginny could say, "I don't mind having sex a little more often. I do love you. But I know I'm just not as revved up as you are. Please understand," then their differences wouldn't sting. But in the end, Ginny is going to have to accept that Hal is more sexed than she, and she'll need to make the effort to make love more often. Hal will have to accept that Ginny's drive is less than his is, and he'll have to learn to live with not having sex as much as he'd like.

Accepting your partner often has a paradoxical side effect. When you stop the persistent effort to get your mate to change and learn to accept him the way he is, he often will make changes along the lines you always wanted.

What Is Acceptance?

Imagine that someone suffered a leg injury that resulted in a permanent limp. Imagine that the individual also happened to be a dancer and the injury put an end to his dance career. If several years later that person was still feeling sorry for himself and angry, or if that person still tried (unsuccessfully) to audition for minor dance parts, we might conclude that he has not accepted his situation. If, however, he pursued a new career—perhaps as a dance instructor or an actor— and if he went on to make a meaningful and happy life despite the fact that he missed dancing, we would say he had accepted his situation.

Acceptance is not grim resignation. It is not tolerating something you can't stand or that is harmful. It is not giving up in defeat. In many ways, it is a peaceful surrender to truth. It is the understanding that some situations or personal characteristics cannot change (much), and it's the willingness to stop insisting that things be what they cannot. In its best form, acceptance is done with respect and love. If you accept a partner's faults and give up a never-ending battle to change him, and if you do so with the love that comes from knowing he has his good qualities, you can make the best of your situation.

The trouble with trying to accept your partner's flaws is that every flaw *appears* changeable. We convince ourselves that it is purely a matter of willpower and that if your mate truly loved you he would persevere and make all the changes you want made. But that is unrealistic and unfair. Often, the partner that won't change has a different set of priorities or values than you do. Maybe he spends money on things you think are foolish but which are important to him. Maybe family get-togethers are not high on your list of exciting events but are high on your partner's list. Maybe you like the yard to look just so and he could care less. You like spontaneity, he likes to make plans in advance. You're sentimental, he won't even shed a tear slicing onions.

Bad habits can be changed. Attitudes can sometimes change. Deeply held values and personality traits are likely to persist. Generally speaking, the longer your partner has acted or thought certain ways, the less likely you will get him to make significant changes in those areas. Nor should you try.

Patty liked Pete's ambitiousness when they met. Pete was a go-getter and wanted to be a success in business. Patty was proud of him. But when they married, his ambitious, never-rest-on-your-laurels approach to his career grew tiresome for her. She wanted him to settle down. He told her he could never be satisfied in his career unless he was always pursuing something bigger and better. Was Patty wrong to want him to change? Yes. Pete's ambitious nature was as much a part of him as his blue eyes. She knew that before she married him. Their main problem was that they never discussed how Patty presumed he would be less ambitious as time went on. That doesn't mean that Pete won't be willing to make some accommodations for her. But he may never change his stripes.

Sandy was introverted and shy. Sid was the life of the party. Sometimes Sandy wished that Sid would lie back and enjoy the quieter side of life and not always have to take center stage. Sid wished that Sandy would loosen up. But they were each smart enough to realize that neither of them could change that drastically. Unless they could learn to live with each other's qualities while occasionally making some sacrifices for each other's sake, their relationship would be unsatisfying.

The value of acceptance is not just that it makes your life easier, but it becomes yet another reason your partner can love you. He knows he's far from perfect and he'll love you for putting up with him.

Talkative people will always have a hard time in a relationship where conversations are kept to a minimum. Less talkative people will have to work at carrying on lengthy conversations. It is less an acquired skill than it is hard wiring. You can force a nonmusical person to learn to play the piano, but she will never be inspired, and she may never be able to play by ear.

Vinnie was raised in a family that yelled a lot. They loved one another, but the volume was always on high. As an adult, he tended to "shoot from the lip" as he liked to say. He'd snap at his wife or his kids, but that was his way. He didn't mean any harm by it. Yes, Vinnie could probably learn to tone it down a bit and learn to listen better. But he will never be a soft-spoken man. It simply is not his nature.

The things you will have to accept about your partner may be annoying or inconvenient but should not be harmful to you. You shouldn't accept abuse, for instance.

But much of the difficulty in learning to accept our partner's less attractive ways is self-induced. When you demand that a partner make changes in ways that are fundamentally incompatible with who he is, you set the stage for an unresolvable, "here we go again" type of argument. Bad feelings will develop on each side. Acceptance, should it ever occur, will feel like defeat instead of an offer of love—which is what it should be.

How to Be More Accepting

Ironically, the ability to be more (or less) accepting of a partner's personality traits is in part a personality trait. Some people, by their nature, are more tolerant and flexible. Others are more intolerant and rigid. A controlling person may resent having to accept another's ways when he wants things done his way. Also, a people-pleasing type of person who is unassertive and always worried about what others think of her may appear to be accepting of her mate's aggravating ways. In reality, she may simply be afraid to confront him. Acceptance motivated by fear is not true acceptance.

Acceptance is a gift to another, not a helpless acquiescence. It is a peace offering. While a person may have no choice but to accept certain events or personality traits, the attitude behind the acceptance is key. That attitude is one of gift giving and honoring, not grudging tolerance.

One cannot teach acceptance, only preach it. (How does one teach how to fall in love or how to forgive?) When a partner accepts you despite your irritating ways, you have a special person in your life. Acceptance does not always come easily. Usually it must be worked on over time.

Acceptance is easier if you consider the following:

- *What qualities has your partner tolerated in you?* When you realize that you are not always a blessing to live with, that you can be mean-spirited or insensitive, you realize the value in acceptance.
- *What benefits does your mate's annoying qualities nevertheless provide for the relationship?* Your differences might complement each other.

    A nontalkative spouse might still be reliable, an anchor in the stormy seas of life. He is quiet, unassuming, and strong in ways you are not—which is probably what attracted you in the first place.

    A bubbly, overemotional spouse may provide you with the emotional expression that you want but cannot express yourself.

    A neat freak makes the house presentable and saves you from tedious housework.

    A spouse who does less housework but who spends her free time being a mom is raising kids who will know they were loved and tended to.

    A quiet and not too sociable spouse helps keep you from spinning out of control with too many responsibilities and social obligations.

    An adventurous partner takes you places you'd never go.

- *Can you detach from your concerns about your mate by focusing on personal areas you'd like to improve or develop a passion for?* If you develop a hobby that inspires you, you may be less concerned about your partner's faults. If you go back to school, make new friends, or read about things you've always wanted to know more about, you will not only become a more interesting person but your need to change your partner may be lessened.

- *Can you try to truly* understand *your partner's reasons for being the way he is, instead of insisting he be something else?* Maybe your not-too-talkative husband grew up in a home where he had to learn to fend for himself emotionally. That doesn't make him a bad person.

> *Sometimes our need to change our mate is based upon dissatisfaction with ourselves. A clue to that is when our partner does change, but we are still not satisfied. Then we should look inward for answers, not outward for blame.*

Phyllis liked the house to be tidy. Her husband, Tom, believed she went overboard and resented it when she complained he wasn't helping out. Each one needed to change a little and be accepting. They achieved it by using what psychologist Neil Jacobson calls "soft emotions." Saying one is hurt, sad, worried, disappointed, or concerned is easier to listen to than hearing words like *angry, enraged, fed up,* or those used to call the other names. "You're right, Tom," Phyllis said. "I do go overboard. But my life seems so cluttered with all my responsibilities to you, the kids, and my job that having an uncluttered house seems important for my peace of mind. All I ask is that you pick up a few of your things at the end of the day."

- *Use humor.* I often suggest to couples that they pick a funny code word (such as Rumpelstiltskin), which informs a partner that he is doing something annoying but which will nonetheless be accepted. For example, if a wife is trying to talk to her husband but he's half-listening while reading the newspaper, she might say, "Rumpelstiltskin." It informs him without complaining, and the use of a funny word makes the moment easy to bear.

Satisfaction in a meaningful relationship comes, at least in part, from knowing that neither partner is perfect and each is nevertheless being loved and (hopefully) cherished despite imperfections. Coming to terms with our loved ones' faults and frailties by accepting some of them shows that we truly love them for who they are.

It's nice to know we've got what it takes.

18
it's not my fault!

Y ou are not always the easiest person to be with, let alone live with.

You know what I'm talking about, don't you? Maybe you haven't noticed certain unflattering qualities about yourself, but other people have noticed. You have your blind spots, but others see you with eyes wide open. Sometimes it's not a pretty sight.

All of us have difficulty seeing our faults clearly. Some people are in complete denial. You ask them to stop being so critical, and they swear they don't have a critical bone in their body. You tell them they always want to get their own way, and they deny they are controlling; they just see their way as the right way.

Many times we know when we've done or said something that was hurtful, but we justify our behavior, make excuses, or defend our intent as noble. We see ourselves not as acting with malice but *reacting* to our partner's hurtful ways. But we fail to see the circular pattern of how hurt in us can prompt us to hurt our partners,

When you have a distorted view of yourself, your view of others will be distorted. You will underreact to others or overreact; you will see virtues when there are none or vices when there are virtues. You may get close, but you will not deeply connect. Your soul yearns to connect with the truth.

which causes more hurt in us, and so on. After a while it doesn't matter who started it. What matters is that the tension or arguments or disagreeable ways of relating are continuing. And *you* share the blame for that. All of your interactions with your mate will result in one of four outcomes:

1. You will get closer to one another.
2. One or both will increase distance (withdraw).
3. You will do battle.
4. There will be no effect one way or the other.

If you are out of touch with your darker side, you will act in ways that promote arguments or withdrawal, but you will not take responsibility for that. Instead, you'll view your mate as difficult, temperamental, cold, or standoffish without having the faintest clue that you are contributing to the problem in a major way.

Of course, your mate is responsible for the problems in your relationship, too. But it is a mistake of the heart when you minimize your faults and see only the faults of your partner. It may make you anxious or guilty to see yourself in a more honest light, but such honesty and devotion to truth is necessary if your relationship is to last.

⚬ facing yourself in the mirror of truth

When you are not fully honest you may admit to faults, but in the same breath you will minimize them. Often, the faults you admit to are the ones that are already a bit extreme and difficult to deny.

> So I drink a little too much. So what? I still earn
>   a great paycheck.
> I know I have a bit of a temper. I can't help it.
> I know I spend money faster than I make it. But
>   it's my outlet. I don't have any other vices.
> I know I've been ignoring you the past two months,
>   but you know how crazy it has been at work.
> Yes, I'm a perfectionist. But maybe you should
>   have high standards, too.

As negative behaviors become less extreme, they are harder for you to notice and own up to. Most of us are much more aware of the impact our mate has on us than we are of the impact we have on our mate. If we were more aware, we'd have to apologize and change.

In your relationship, do you ever:

- Find fault, even over little things you could easily overlook? (*You left the light on in the kitchen all night, Sue.*)
- Make agreements you know you may be unable to keep?
- Tolerate behavior you dislike, then act like a martyr?
- Make slight put-downs of your spouse to others? (*Hank has his unromantic side, believe me.*)
- Disagree with your mate using polite words, but in a tone that tells her she's an idiot?
- Get very defensive at the slightest complaint and thereby shut down further conversation? (*Well, how was I supposed to know that the car was due for an oil change?*)
- Sulk, and then when your partner asks what's wrong, you let him have it?
- Claim (falsely, or with exaggeration) that you don't know how to do certain things so that your mate must do them for you? (Such as change a diaper, use a weed trimmer, call a repair service, etc.)
- Complain that your mate doesn't help out but then criticize her when she does or tell her, "Never mind, I'll do it!"
- Assist your mate on some task but do so in a careless way, then get mad if she complains that you're no help at all?
- Show anger at your mate over something not her fault? (*I didn't like the way that man was looking at you. Why did you have to smile at him when you were introduced?*)
- Make your spouse the "bad guy" to the kids? (*No, we can't go to the amusement park. Your dad says it's too expensive.*)
- Pooh-pooh your mate's ideas and dreams? (*You want to go back to school? Yeah, right. I can see you now freaking out over your first test.*)
- Routinely keep quiet about something important because you want to be nice? (You'll grow resentful over time and your partner won't have the slightest idea why.)
- Frequently turn down suggestions to do something fun because you are too tired?

- Want to be an involved parent but only deal with the kids on your terms—when you're ready, when you're not busy with other things, when you're not tired . . . ?
- Buy something expensive you want without discussing it, but get angry if your mate buys something far less expensive?

The list can go on. If you don't think you ever act in any of those ways, ask your partner what he thinks. (If you get angry at his answer, then add to the above list of annoying traits: gets mad when asks for—and receives—an honest opinion.)

Why You Do What You Do

Arguments, crankiness, or thoughtless acts sometimes happen for obvious and understandable reasons. An exhausting day at work, high stress, or many worries can make us overreact to situations and become difficult to live with. It's also common for misunderstandings to lead to unnecessary conflicts. And many frustrated partners act in ways they think will solve a relationship problem but which actually make it worse. For example:

- A wife spends more time on the job because her relationship with her husband has grown tense. That only increases the emotional distance between them.
- A man tunes out the woman in his life when she talks because he thinks she is too critical. She gets angry that he isn't listening and criticizes him.
- A man tries to show his new companion that he is flexible and unselfish by saying things such as, "I don't care what we do this weekend. You choose." Unfortunately, he comes across as indifferent and unenthusiastic, which leads to conflict.
- A wife thinks her second husband is too harsh with her children, so she is lenient with them to compensate. The man feels undermined and misunderstood, so he is more likely to react harshly the next time the kids misbehave.

But many of our unflattering and unhelpful ways of relating are formed from our childhood. We use our original family as the blueprint for how to respond in a romantic relationship. We want to repeat those patterns we liked, and change those patterns we disliked. Unfortunately, the more negative our experiences were growing up, the more difficulty we have judging our current relationship accurately. It's easy to think you have overcome a hurtful or difficult past. Perhaps your father was an alcoholic and you don't drink. But you have a higher chance of linking up with someone who does drink or who has some addiction problem.

Maybe one parent was emotionally absent and you craved attention and affection but rarely received it. You may grow up craving affection from your partner, but you may smother your partner in the process or you may be distant and unable to show as much affection.

Maybe you had little money growing up. You may spend money freely now, or you may have learned the value of a dollar and tend to save instead of spend.

Maybe a worrisome, overprotective parent raised you. You may seek out a partner you can grow dependent on and who will take care of you, or you may want to maintain a high degree of independence from your mate.

Maybe your parents were critical and hard to satisfy. You may do the same to your kids, or you may marry someone who is critical. Or, you will feel criticized even when your mate is simply offering a different point of view.

WHAT WAS YOUR ROLE IN YOUR FAMILY GROWING UP?

Were you the perfect child who never wanted to cause trouble? Were you the family's therapist or peacemaker? Were you the troublemaker who always called negative attention to yourself? Were you the caretaker for your younger siblings? Were you a parent's confidant? Were you spoiled? Were you over-responsible? Chances are you will re-create the role you played in childhood within your marriage, even if you are trying hard not to.

WHAT DO YOU WISH YOU RECEIVED
FROM YOUR CHILDHOOD BUT DIDN'T?

Did you want to be taken seriously? Appreciated? Protected? Loved? Given more independence? Did you want to feel safer? Did you want more recognition or a sense of accomplishment? More fair treatment? Did you wish you had more of a childhood instead of having to grow up too fast? Any unmet needs will show up on the doorstep of your romantic relationships, especially your marriage.

If you are unhappy or dissatisfied in your current relationship, the chances are good that what's missing now is what was missing from your childhood. But what's important to realize is that you, much more than your partner, are responsible for why you are unhappy. You are re-creating your role from childhood or you are tolerating unacceptable behavior because of low self-esteem that originated from your past, or you are misunderstanding the nature of your current problems. (By the way, your partner is probably doing the same thing.)

Nick grew up in an unfriendly, unaffectionate household. He never felt truly loved or respected. Now in his second marriage, his wife, Gloria, frustrates him. She seems to criticize him for no good reason or grow impatient when he doesn't do things in a manner she likes. So he pulls away from her and once again he is in an unaffectionate household. Gloria had a similar background. Her mother was an alcoholic and her father dealt with the problem by working as many hours as he could. Gloria was the oldest child and had to run the household for her mother. She craves attention and affection from Nick, but he doesn't offer it. She compensates by trying to keep the house clean and tidy (it's an old way of coping and at least she can feel good about her cleaning skills), but then she gets angry when he is careless or sloppy. He thinks she's too critical. She thinks he doesn't care about her feelings. The more she criticizes, the more he pulls away and the more she focuses on keeping the house in tip-top shape. Then she feels neglected as she did as a child. She tries to invite closeness by initiating conversations that end up with him being uncommunicative. To feel better, she asks him to help out with chores. He complies but messes up and she criticizes him (*Can't you just do what I ask? Why must you always be careless about things that are important to me?*). The pattern continues.

What could they do to get out of their self-imposed trap?

1. Each must first examine how they are complicating the situation. They need to stop blaming the partner and start examining their own role in the problem. Gloria must realize that criticizing Nick—however legitimate—only pushes him away. Nick must realize that shutting down during conversation or being careless about chores aggravates Gloria.

2. Each must realize that they have mixed feelings about closeness. They want it, but they do not trust it. That means that as much as they will act in ways to invite closeness, they will also act in ways that repel closeness. Usually, one will invite closeness just at the time the other is not ready.

3. They must realize that their partner can never make up for what was lost during childhood. Nick and Gloria each feel needy. Even when they respond well to each other, the hole from their past does not get filled. They interpret that as a sign that their partner did not do enough. In reality, their partner could never do enough.

4. A helpful task is for them to take daily turns initiating affection, intimacy, or a pleasurable joint activity (taking a walk, cuddling, giving back rubs, and so on). Nick might initiate on odd days of the month, Gloria on even days. There must be a preagreement that the noninitiator must respond positively to the overture and must go along with whatever the other is requesting. If those rules are followed, it makes it impossible for each one to be out of sync with the other. Over time, the couple will be more comfortable giving and receiving affection or spending intimate moments together, and the day-on/day-off rule can be put aside.

5. Another helpful task is to assume that their frustration with each other is really based on a frustration from their past. Instead of criticizing or complaining, they can say: "Maybe you aren't being cold or rejecting just now. Maybe I'm overreacting because of my past. What could we each do today that will make us feel loved and appreciated?"

6. A third task is for each to draw up a list of at least ten small activities that their partner could do that would make them feel more special or make their day go easier. For example, Nick could list things such as: Welcome me home with a kiss and a warm hug; vacuum out my car; sometimes give me twenty minutes to unwind after work before you expect me to be fully available to you. Gloria might list things such as: Call me during the day to say hi; once in a while give me a compliment; hold my hand when we're strolling in the mall; put the dirty dishes in the dishwasher before going to bed. They should exchange the lists and clarify any ambiguous requests. Then they should try to perform at least one thing from their partner's list every day, in addition to positive things they would ordinarily do. That will add a minimum of sixty positive gestures per month, which will definitely improve the atmosphere at home.

7. A final task is for each to list two or three behaviors that the other one does that are highly toxic or hurtful. The goal is to reduce the frequency of such toxic behaviors. Doing something hurtful costs much more than doing something kind, so it requires many kind acts to make up for one hurtful act.

～

Looking at your role in any problem will always pay dividends, as long as there is a basis of love and caring in the relationship.

19

it's just between the three of us

When a relationship problem persists despite determined efforts to solve it, or when personal symptoms (anxiety, depression, reduced ambition, problems in school, etc.) persist, chances are that something is being overlooked. Often, that something is what is known in psychology as "emotional triangles." A triangle exists when the tension between two people gets so high that one of the partners focuses on a third person to divert their anxiety. This has the effect of lowering tension but ignoring the relationship problem. The most common triangle among couples is the child-focused triangle. Here, the dissatisfied partner (usually the wife) gets overinvolved in her children's lives because her marriage is unhappy (a dissatisfied husband is more likely to spend more time at work or out of the house, not with his kids). Soon, the husband feels like an outsider. He might complain about being ignored. His wife will dismiss his complaints as either selfish or shortsighted (*Can't you see I have to spend time with the kids?*) and continue to pull away from him. Eventually their relationship is even less satisfying and the wife must continue to devote energy to her children because they are her main source of fulfillment. The triangle (wife-children-husband) has now hardened. Originally it helped

The main consequence of emotional triangles is that they perpetuate the status quo and block change.

the wife feel less stressed from her marriage. Now it was keeping her marriage from improving.

The reason triangles form is because they tend to *lower* anxiety at first. But as you will soon see, lowering stress by forming an emotional triangle is a mistake of the heart. While it reduces anxiety in the short run, emotional triangles prevent problems from being resolved. Then the anxiety that results from having a persistent, unresolved problem causes partners to make more emotional triangles. Like an addict who cannot tolerate withdrawal symptoms and who must therefore use more of the substance that he wishes to withdraw from, couples keep emotional triangles alive and wonder why some of their problems never go away.

∾ keep others out of the middle of your relationship

Emotional triangles are extremely common and need not be toxic. But they must not be overlooked, otherwise you run a risk of keeping some problems alive or starting new problems. When Dan and Laura began having some difficulties in communication, Dan confided in his best friend, Steve. What began as a reasonable effort by Steve to be a confidant to Dan resulted in a relationship impasse between Laura and Dan. Asking Steve for advice was not a problem. The problem was that over time Dan spoke less and less to Laura about his relationship issues and more and more to Steve. Half the time Laura didn't even know Dan was upset about something because he only spoke of it with Steve. Soon, Steve commented that perhaps Dan and Laura's relationship was a mistake. Believing that Steve might be right, Dan pulled further away from Laura emotionally and their problems only worsened—which made him want to confide more in Steve.

Imagine that Dan never consulted with Steve. Imagine instead that Laura consulted with her parents. What began as parents simply being supportive resulted in Laura talking with them almost daily, giving them updates and revealing certain intimacies that Dan would have been upset to learn she had disclosed. Imagine Dan complaining to Laura that she is too involved with her parents or that her parents should "mind their own business." Laura does not want to keep her folks out of the loop because they have become her lifeline to emotional stability. Without them she'd be floundering. So she yells at Dan that just because he isn't as close to his parents as she is with hers is no reason to keep her away from them. Dan walks away in a huff and Laura has one more incident to report to her parents.

In each of the above examples two things happened. A triangle formed and the emotional distance between the couple lengthened, while at the same time the distance between one of them and their confidant (Dan and Steve or Laura and her parents) diminished. An emotional triangle does not mean that a three-some exists. It means that two people become more closely aligned against a third. If a wife is aligned with her parents against her husband, or if a husband is aligned with his oldest child against his wife, or if a woman is aligned with her lover against her husband, an emotional triangle has formed and has begun preventing positive change from happening.

As a rule of thumb, you should talk to a friend or family member about your relationship problems only if you are willing to talk to your mate about those issues even more often. Otherwise, you run a huge risk of alienating your partner from you even further. Family and friends are not always objective and neither are you.

Relationships Should Be Twosomes, Not Threesomes

Emotional triangles exist everywhere. Imagine you are at a party where you know only a few people and you are in a conversation with someone you'd rather not spend any more time with. You might just excuse yourself and leave. Or, you might feign an illness or say you have to use the bathroom. Or you might wave to a friend and then excuse yourself. Any of these ways helps you to reduce discomfort. When you are in a relationship and the tension gets too high, you only have a few choices (other than ending the relationship). You can discuss the tension and hopefully relieve it. You can pretend the tension is not so bad and look forward to some alone time later on. Or, you can create an emotional triangle. Routinely turning on the TV to avoid dinner conversation forms a type of triangle, and the third point in the triangle is an inanimate object. Sometimes the third point could be a physical symptom.

Paige was unhappily married to Pete for almost twenty years. Pete was loud and disagreeable and often drank too much. Paige had an anxiety disorder where she had a hard time driving by herself because of panic attacks. While Pete paid little attention to Paige most of the time, he was forced to pay attention to her when her panic attacks became severe. (When he didn't, she called an ambulance fearing that her panic would cause a heart attack.) In therapy, Paige complained about her husband yet had to admit he was always there for her "when I needed him the most." In a way, her anxiety was the third point in the triangle. She and her husband united against the panic disorder. Of course, after her attack had passed, Pete would be furious with Paige for being such an "emotional basket case" and he'd withdraw from her. Eventually, another attack would bring the couple together.

Ramon dealt with his dissatisfaction with his partner by spending more time fantasizing about the ideal woman. A harmless act at first, Ramon would retreat to this fantasy more and more instead of dealing with his relationship concerns more directly.

Colin coped with his relationship problems not by facing them squarely but by smoking pot. Getting high allowed Colin to "be there and not be there" at the same time. He'd be alone with his wife but detached enough to be less bothered by their problems.

Both Ramon and Colin found a way to cope with their concerns but in a manner that prevented problems from being resolved.

Three's a Crowd: How to Dismantle Emotional Triangles

A person who is hooked on painkillers must eventually learn to cope with pain using ways other than drugs. Similarly, a person in an emotional triangle must learn to deal with relationship pain without bringing in a third person. That is a difficult process. Triangles are emotionally driven, and most people try to avoid emotional pain whenever possible. Actually, since emotional triangles tend to preserve the status quo, removing triangles can disrupt the status quo. (Many people worry that changing the status quo risks ending the relationship.)

For example, Clyde was a respected politician with two children. He was unhappy in his marriage but could not imagine ending it. He began an affair with a married woman who also did not want her marriage to end. His affair helped him to tolerate his wife (since he coped with his marital distress by looking forward to being with the other woman) and made him happier. His marriage was salvaged (though somewhat empty), and his reputation as a married man was left intact. For Clyde to end his affair he'd have to find a way to improve his marriage or to end it. Neither option excited him.

Sally was a devoted mother, in part because she was emotionally distant from her partner, the man she had been living with the past ten years. Her children were her life. She complained that Harry never took an interest in her or his children, so she doted on them and was pained that Harry was so distant. Still, Harry finally said he wanted to be more a part of Sally's life. In therapy, they agreed to try to improve their relationship. But when Harry tried to spend time with Sally alone, she always complained that the kids were being ignored. When Harry tried to spend more time with the kids, Sally complained that he didn't know how best to entertain them. The triangle—with Sally and the kids aligned against Harry— was a stubborn one. To change it, Sally would have to face two fears. First, she feared an empty void would open up if she was less involved with her kids. That was the only fulfilling role she had in life. Second, she feared that greater involvement with Harry would result in heartbreak later on (her first marriage ended in failure). She preferred the status quo.

Once a triangle has become chronic, you cannot escape it without facing some kind of personal anxiety or pain. And yet, if you hope to be truly happy in your relationship, you must.

The best way to get out of a triangle is to never get in one in the first place, even though others may be trying to get you into a triangle. An example every parent can relate to occurs when bickering children try to get a parent to be judge and jury and resolve a sibling argument. (Unfortunately, the siblings have their own idea of who is right and do not want objectivity.) Every parent has broken up an argument among kids. But if the pattern becomes repetitive, then a triangle has formed. Usually, the parent in the middle takes on more anxiety and gets stressed out. (Sound familiar?) But coming to the children's rescue in that way does not teach kids to resolve their own problems. Most parents do the right thing when they learn to step back and eventually allow their kids to solve their own problems, at least most of the time.

Another example might be that your mother, unhappy in her own marriage, confides in you. Wanting to be a supportive son or daughter, you listen. But soon you start to feel angry at the other parent or perhaps disloyal. Now you are feeling stressed and may try to avoid picking up the phone when you think your mom is calling to complain again.

How do you stay out of the middle? You can *try* not to take sides, but often the other person is exceedingly good at dragging you in. Your best bet is to assert yourself and refuse to get involved.

"Mom, I love you and I'm sorry you and Dad aren't getting along. But these phone calls make me upset and there is nothing I can do. So from now on you'll have to discuss other things." Of course, Mom will persist. Then you have two choices (and you must do one of them if you wish to get out of the triangle).

CHOICE ONE: Say, "Mom, if you insist on talking about Dad, I will hang up." (You must hang up if she continues.)

CHOICE TWO: "Mom, I'm going to speak to Dad and ask him why you are telling me all these things instead of telling him." (Then you must find a way to tell your father that. This choice can be hard to do but often works the best.)

But what if *you* are the one who is triangling in others? First, you must discover what triangles you have formed. Then you must notice who you are aligned with and who you are distant from. Then (sounds simple, but it's difficult to do) you must reverse the polarity. You must move closer to the person you've been distant from, and farther from the person you've been too close to. For example, a mom overinvolved with her kids and underinvolved with her husband must spend more time with her husband doing pleasant things, and must spend less time with her children. If a dad was underinvolved with his wife and kids but overinvolved with work, he must spend fewer hours at work and more hours with his family. If you confide too much in your friend (or even your therapist) but spend little time with your mate, you must reverse the trend.

Backlash

Backlash is what you can expect when you try to unhook yourself from an emotional triangle. Since triangles reduce tension by siphoning off energy into a third person, breaking up a triangle will put anxiety back where it belongs—between the couple. A mom who reverses direction and spends more time with her husband now and less with her kids cannot be expected to be immediately happy and content with the arrangement. She will worry about the children and find fault with her mate. The children may not like it, either. They may sense the tension between the couple and respond with their own anxiety or disruptive behavior. If the mom responds by paying more attention to them and less to her husband, the old triangle has resurfaced. Or perhaps the husband will respond to the added attention his wife is giving him by being anxious and uncommunicative. That may prompt his wife to say "Why bother?" and revert to the former relationship pattern.

You must predict ahead of time what upsetting things might happen after you unhook yourself from a triangle. Then you must plan what you can do that will not reform the old triangle.

TYPICAL RESPONSES AFTER YOU UNHOOK A TRIANGLE

These reactions may be mild or intense. They will subside. However, until they do subside the members of the triangle may feel more discomfort.

- Anger
- Acting out
- Anxiety
- A sense that the new pattern is unnatural and uncomfortable (and therefore, you may wrongly conclude, it should not continue)
- Provoking arguments
- Giving up quickly when the new pattern doesn't feel good right away
- A rise in physical or emotional symptoms (panic, depression, chest pain, backaches, dizziness, migraines, allergies, a sense of loss, a disrupted sense of meaning to one's life, substance use, and so on)

It is not uncommon that when a person tries to unhook themselves from a triangle, someone else has a major crisis that compels the person to reactivate the triangle. For example, when an adult son was in the middle of his parents' unhappy marriage, he told his parents he would no longer be their confidant. A few days later his father was rushed to the hospital with chest pain. He was diagnosed with treatable angina. But the crisis prompted the young man to reestablish his role as his parents' confidant.

Similarly, a woman who was having an affair chose to end it and focus instead on rebuilding her marriage. When her lover was in a car accident two weeks later, she reconnected with him—intending it to be temporary—but found herself still connected two months later.

As you can see, once a triangle is disconnected the couple must be ready to work on their relationship and not allow the expected backlash to throw them off course. Neither must they assume that any backlash means that a partner must be disinterested in working things out. Backlash is automatic.

∼

The more emotionally healthy a person, the easier it will be to unhook from a triangle. But once a triangle has formed, it never goes away entirely. It may be disconnected, but it exists ready to reconnect if the emotional climate requires it. You are in the best position if you try to face your relationship issues squarely and resolve them, or at least learn to accept some differences. The minute you start involving others to compensate for your anxiety or unhappiness, you risk making your problems resistant to change.

That's a mistake of the heart you can avoid if you try. The first step is becoming aware that emotional triangles exist. Now you are.

20
I want to be in love again

Fred wondered if he'd ever find the right woman. He was a quiet sort, a good listener, but not much of a talker. He enjoyed peaceful pursuits such as astronomy and visiting art galleries. He recently purchased his own home and discovered that he liked landscaping, too. He wasn't looking hard for a mate, so he was surprised when Marcia simply appeared, almost out of nowhere. He met her in the checkout line at the drugstore. They struck up a conversation. They accompanied each other outside and laughed when they saw that they had parked right next to each other. Then he noticed that one of her tires was low on air. She seemed distressed, more than she should have been for such a small thing. He told her to follow him and he drove to a convenience store that had an air hose outside. He even paid the fifty cents it cost to start the machine since she didn't have any loose change. She offered to buy him lunch. From then on they spoke every day and got together as often as possible.

Marcia was recently separated, but she knew the marriage was over. She wanted out. Fred was delighted at his good fortune. Marcia was easy to be with and she didn't demand that he be a great conversationalist, as many of his ex-girlfriends had. Ironically, he talked a lot with Marcia. He had never opened up to anyone this much before.

Marcia and Fred deserved to be happy, didn't they? Was this really good timing? Or were Marcia and Fred making a stupid mistake?

℘ take time to feel and heal

If Marcia were smart, she would have avoided any new intimate relationships for a while. And if Fred were smart, he'd have acted more low-key with Marcia instead of quickly placing her at the center of his life. Their mistake was that they led with their hearts. Their mutual desire to feel cared about, attractive, and needed made them overlook the obvious: Marcia was still reeling from a dissolving marriage. The odds that this relationship would last were low. But the strong emotional impact of having someone appreciate them turned their minds into mush. Fred always had a tendency to attract needy women. If he ever examined that fact, he'd realize that Marcia was not too different from all the others (she felt helpless when her tire went flat). But his heart spoke louder than his good sense.

When you are recovering from a relationship breakup, when your esteem is fragile, and when your hope for a bright future feels dim, you are emotionally vulnerable to anybody who shows caring or concern.

During emotionally arduous times, we bond with people we might not otherwise bond with. If you look at your friends (old and new) who have meant the most to you, you will see that many of them were your companions during some ordeal. You went to high school together while the perils of adolescence were all around you. Or you served in the military together. Or you were neighbors at the time you each gave birth to your first child and learned how to cope with motherhood at the same time. These relationships may be meaningful and long-lasting. But finding the person to spend your life with requires more than a heartfelt connection. It requires some wisdom to discern if you are truly meant for one another.

The Hard Facts

The truth is that most people require about one to two years after a breakup from a significant relationship before they are emotionally ready to start fresh. Obviously, some people are ready to move on much earlier, some take even longer, but the more intense and important your relationship was, the more likely you'll need at least a year to put your head and heart in proper working order. Anything less and you are making a serious mistake of the heart. One of the reasons the divorce rate is higher the second time around (62 percent at the low end) is that people try to find new love when they haven't recovered from the love they lost.

People involved in an extramarital affair prior to the breakup of their marriage are particularly at risk for making a mistake of the heart—if they hope to remain with their lover. They are already off and running, trying to juggle two relationships. After a divorce, the couple who had the affair ends up together only about 10 percent of the time, but many of these couples think their odds of success are higher.

The affair that ends a marriage usually ends after the marriage is over.

But perhaps you think that your affair was different. Perhaps you fell in love with the other person and ended your marriage so you two could be together. The awful truth is that affair relationships rarely lead to happily-ever-after relationships, even when the couple seems desperate to make it happen. Why? Two reasons predominate:

1. *The passion of an affair is often fueled by artificial heat.* Such passion feeds on the drama that secrecy brings: sending coded messages on a pager to your lover; lying to your mate with clever stories; rushing through a lunch hour to make voracious love in a motel room; letting his phone ring once to let him know you made it safely home without being discovered; doing something "naughty" that you know many friends or relatives would disapprove of. When the marriage is finished and the affair is public, the drama subsides. What once was an obsessive preoccupation and a heart-pounding thriller of secret union evolves into the equivalent of walking through an amusement park haunted mansion with the lights turned on. What seemed so deep, dark, and exciting is now a room full of trick mirrors.

2. *The positive aspects of the affair were judged only in the context of the negative aspects of the failing marriage.* Just about anything tastes better than a marriage gone sour. When the marriage is clearly over, however, the affair relationship must now stand on its own. Qualities of your partner that were so pleasant and comforting compared to your ex's may in reality be something less than you want. Now you expect more.

Stan and Thelma carried on a twenty-year affair while each was married. They loved their mates, but they loved each other, too. Neither wanted to break up their families, so they agreed to meet in secret and did so for two decades. Thelma was initially shocked when her husband asked for a divorce after their last child left home, but she wasn't surprised. After her divorce she continued to secretly see Stan. When Stan's wife died suddenly of a brain aneurysm, Thelma was sure that she and Stan would eventually marry. But within six months of his wife's death, Stan called a halt to his affair with Thelma. Thelma was confused and shaken, but Stan was adamant. He couldn't explain the reasons why, but he just felt differently toward her. Four years later Stan did remarry. But it wasn't to Thelma.

This outcome is not too surprising. Thelma and Stan's affair was kept alive more for the two reasons stated above than it was kept alive by deep, committed love. They just never realized it before.

Fools Rush In

When a meaningful relationship ends, it takes time and honesty to examine the reasons why. But people who rush into another relationship are not taking the time and are probably kidding themselves about the reasons for the breakup.

Breakups, separations, and divorce are painful. How do people cope with the pain? Constantly thinking about the relationship means that your mind has not fully comprehended what happened. You are in shock and have to review the same material until it finally sinks in. You are probably still desperate for reconciliation. When reality finally hits, it is accompanied by distortion. You pretend that the relationship really didn't matter (as a way to dull the pain) or you pretend that your ex was primarily at fault for its failure. Even people who believe the breakup was all their fault due to their inadequacy still lash out at their ex, blaming them for not persevering. This emotional upheaval places you at disadvantage when you try to start a new relationship too soon. If you feel worthless and unlovable (or self-righteously angry), all it takes is someone taking a keen interest in you and you will begin to perk up. You'll realize that you are not a complete disaster of a person and you'll begin to focus on

You repair emotional wounds by grieving the loss, figuring where you went wrong, forgiving, and paving a new road to your future. That simply takes time and freedom from the distractions that a new lover brings.

flaws your ex possessed. You may even get a lot of sympathy, especially if your new date likes you. Feeling much better, you'll want to keep dating. Who wouldn't? Dating is not the risk, but falling in love too quickly is. Dating is important as long as you don't rush into anything. It makes you realize that life goes on and that you still have appeal. But your energy is best spent repairing your emotional wounds.

If you are thrilled to end your old relationship, you are still at a major disadvantage if you jump right into a new relationship. You are under the illusion that you simply had picked the wrong person before, but now you believe your judgment is honed. If you rush in, you will likely repeat mistakes you made before—mistakes you are ignoring because you need to feel on top of your game. Besides, you may still have to deal with the leftovers—arguments over bills, separation agreements, visitation (even couples without kids want to visit their pets once in a while). You're not ready yet to invest fully in a new person.

When you ignore past mistakes, you are likely to repeat them. Even if you seek a new partner who possesses many qualities your old mate never possessed, you still must proceed slowly and let your thoughts and feelings reorganize themselves. Your new mate will inevitably say or do something reminiscent of your old partner. Then your emotions will fly like particles in a snow globe. More important, research shows that it is not differences between partners that make a difference, but how a couple manages conflict. If you manage conflict ineffectively, it doesn't really matter what qualities your new mate possesses.

Lessons of Grief

The relationship that ended was meaningful, however poorly it ended. It used to be the light that woke you every morning, winked at you during the day, and warmed you to sleep every night. It was part of your identity. You thought in terms of "us," not just "me." You and your former partner may have had children together. You certainly had dreams, some of which may have come true. Even if you're happy to be rid of your ex, you need to grieve the loss of old dreams, the family breakup, and years of your life that you wonder if you wasted. You owe it to yourself and to your future partner to properly grieve. How do you do that?

First, don't be afraid of feeling sad or very angry. You won't always feel this way, but for now and for many months you probably will. It is a measure not so much of what you lost—though that is certainly part of it—but a measure of what you loved (or wanted to love).

Grief is a form of giving back. It is realizing that people we love are not ours to keep. As such, every relationship is precious because it is temporary. Sooner or later, for one reason or another, it comes to an end (at least on earth). You grieve by remembering the good times and the hard times. You recall the qualities of your partner that first attracted you. You recall the great expectations and the eventual letdown. You grieve by doing some soul searching and identifying your mistakes. If you do this to berate yourself, it will achieve nothing. Anger is a common part of the grief process, but berating yourself is extreme. Acknowledge your mistakes, but don't criticize your whole personhood. You are not worthless or unlovable. You participated in a relationship that didn't work out. People make mistakes out of fear or ignorance, not because they are worthless.

There is no cookbook formula for making the transition from one relationship to the next. Someone who left their partner emotionally a year or more before the actual breakup is operating on a different time frame than someone who was taken by surprise when their mate suddenly walked out. But the following checklist might help. You are probably ready to date seriously when:

- About a year has passed since your marriage (or other *significant* relationship) ended. If your ex was verbally or physically abusive or was an alcoholic, you need more time.
- You find yourself thinking much more often about your future than your past.
- You have focused on self-improvement for six to nine months. That might include an exercise program, returning to school, more time with friends, or new hobbies.
- You can identify where you went wrong and why.
- Your attitude toward your ex-partner is a sincere "I wish him [or her] well."
- You're eager for a new relationship but not desperate or lonely.
- You feel anchored in your role as a parent. Parenting may be more exhausting and stressful, but by the end of the day you should believe you are a good and dedicated mom or dad.
- Trusted friends (known for their good judgment) tell you they think you are ready.

Even if you think you are ready, think twice about investing in a new relationship if:

- You are still preoccupied with your ex's behavior or attitudes.
- You tend to depend a lot on others' approval for your self-worth.
- You have yet to establish a workable routine to your daily life.
- You allow others to hurt you when you could speak up and stop it.
- You are so overcommitted with your time that you haven't faced your loss.
- You have a hard time making decisions.
- You've had a string of bad relationships. (Talk to a professional.)

It can be extremely helpful to write out your feelings and concerns every day for at least twenty minutes. Research by Dr. James Pennebaker has shown that this is a catalyst for healing, much more than using the same time to simply think about matters. If you allow a close friend to read your journal, the benefits may be even greater. Try it for two weeks. The results may surprise you.

If you are newly involved with someone who recently ended a long-term relationship, you are probably helping the person cope. But if your hope is to achieve a meaningful, committed relationship, you will have to be patient and realize that things may not work out in the long run. Your new love is viewing you in the context of his former lover. She is an invisible but ever present person in his life, even when he's in bed with you.

There are risks when you fall in love with someone who has not yet come to terms with his last effort at love. Proceed gently and with eyes wide open.

As a final thought, consider this: People tend to attract—and be attracted to—people who are at the same level of psychological development and adjustment as themselves. Your actions or symptoms may be different from his (you're a rescuer, he's feeling helpless; he's a workaholic, you're laid back; and so on), but in the school of psychological development you're both in the same grade. If on a scale of one to ten your current level of adjustment after the breakup is a five or six, you will not attract someone who is at an eight or higher. If you do, he won't stick around. If you are in a weakened emotional state, the next person you get seriously involved with will also be weak (even if he seems strong). Now you two have to struggle together and you'll probably trip over each other. Focus on your own healing and self-improvement, get promoted to a higher grade, and then go out and attract someone who is more emotionally together.

mistakes of the soul

21

what does spirituality have to do with my relationship?

C an true, deep, devotional love be completely understood without an understanding of God? Can human love be reduced to chemicals and biology, or is there something more? Does love spring from our soul?

The elderly couple came into my office. She pushed him in his wheelchair, though at age seventy she was far from strong. Because of an accident, the husband was confined to the chair. He was able to get up, with difficulty, but walking was very painful and usually impossible. As they spoke, what became obvious to me was the depth of love the couple had for one another. They were old and infirm, they lived by themselves, yet their life together seemed a blessing to them. It pained her deeply to see him in a wheelchair because he had always been an active man, a laborer by trade. But on some occasions she had found him crumpled to the floor after an unsuccessful attempt to walk. He risked a more serious injury and she was frightened, so frightened he would hurt himself even more. Could I help him to accept his condition?

In listening to their story, their lifetime of love and sacrifice for one another, I was not surprised by their ultimate decision on what to do.

"After listening to my wife speak to you," the old man said, "I realize that I have been selfish trying to walk when I know I can't. I will only make my wife worry and she doesn't deserve that." He turned to look at her and smiled. "You don't have to worry," he said. "I will stay in my chair." He clasped her hand. "I owe you that."

Then his wife spoke up. "After listening to my husband, I realize that *I* have been selfish. Yes, I worry about him getting hurt. But I know that he needs to keep trying to walk, even if it means he will hurt himself. My husband has never been a quitter. He has always been determined. I cannot take that away from him when he has had his legs taken from him." Then she turned to him and spoke. "It's okay if you try to walk whenever you want. I understand." She had tears in her eyes but tried to keep her husband from seeing her weep.

They thanked me for my help and left.

Could a scientist explain their love by reducing it to a biochemical process of the brain? No. Their love transcended the physical realm. Theirs was a highly spiritual love.

∾ believe in something greater than yourself

The word *psychology* literally means the study of the soul. However, in this day and age it has come to mean something less: the study of behavior, the study of attitudes, the study of emotions, and so forth. Just as medieval physicians chopped up a body in order to locate the soul, and thereby lost both, psychologists and mental health professionals often treat people—perhaps with compassion—but with little or no regard to their spiritual dimension. And yet the spiritual dimension is not only the glue that binds all other facets of the human being, it is the dimension that most directly cries out when a person sits in a therapist's office. While people go to therapy to heal a multitude of problems, there are—in the final analysis—only four:

1. How can I experience love in my life?
2. How can I overcome fear?
3. How can I make my life meaningful and fulfilling (despite loss)?
4. How can I find peace of mind?

Each of those issues is fundamentally spiritual in nature. While the hard-core scientifically minded therapist may view treatment as a nonspiritual process (and perhaps as solely a biological process where medications are prescribed), I would argue that treatment is most meaningful when it taps the spiritual dimension, regardless of the therapist's intent.

Marriage can be looked upon as many things. Rarely does a couple view it primarily as a spiritual union. Instead, it is viewed as a socially proscribed union and a physical union. The couple lives together, sets up house, probably has children, and attempts to create a family unit that will (hopefully) bring about happiness and fulfillment. When a couple looks at marriage without regard to its spiritual dimension, however, the chance for family breakup rises. Of course, many spiritual and religious couples divorce, and nonreligious couples may spend a lifetime together. Spirituality does not ensure marital bliss. But on average, the more spiritual a person is and the more religion plays a role in his or her life, the greater the odds the marriage will last and be fulfilling.

> *Research shows that highly religious people who have lasting marriages are not staying together primarily because they believe that divorce is wrong. They are genuinely happier and have a more satisfying sex life, too.*

Seeking Spirituality in an Age of Self

"What helped me become more spiritual and go back to church was becoming a mother," Charlotte said. "Until then I guess I always believed in God, but God was not a part of my everyday life. Don't get me wrong. I tried to be a good person. But I didn't pray all that much and I rarely went to church. But by the time my kids were attending school, I realized I wanted them to believe in God and I knew that the only way I could do that was to change my lifestyle and *show* them—not just tell them—that I believed in God, too."

Charlotte's story is typical. There is something so mystical and spiritual about having and raising children that it becomes difficult to ignore the spiritual side of life that parenthood reveals.

Mike became a father for the first time at age fifty. It was his second marriage and the prospect of fatherhood scared him. He envisioned a messy household, sleepless nights, and financial disarray. He had planned on retiring at age fifty-five, but that was no longer possible. But when his daughter arrived he experienced a transformation like no other. The love he felt for his daughter was so deep and intense he was taken aback by its strength. "It was like a piece of heaven had literally fallen into my lap," he said.

It is not surprising that when a man's seed is planted inside a woman, a seed of faith is also planted. So many parents discover that they are not only better people for having raised a child, they are more spiritual as well.

Couples without children can certainly live beautifully spiritual lives (and having children is no ticket to a spiritual life—the statistics on child abuse attest to that). But children provide, at least for most couples, a more direct path to their soul. If you ask an average, happily married person if he would give up his life for his spouse, he would probably say yes after a moment's hesitation. Ask that same person if he would give up his life to save his child and he would answer yes with no hesitation. The experience of such a profound form of love (spouse to spouse, but especially parent to child) is so overwhelming to us, that most loving parents and spouses retreat to a mind-set where day-to-day hassles can get in the way of showing our love to those we say we love. We get angry with our kids for spilling milk on the couch. We yell at them if they make us late for an appointment. Our mate's annoying habits irritate us and we give them ugly glances. We search for moments where we can get away from our loved ones and find some solitude. It is almost as if we cannot tolerate the experience of intense love for very long. We have to dilute it with anger, selfishness, or materialistic pursuits. Why?

Perhaps the answer lies in the spiritual realm. Those deeply felt moments of devotional love toward a spouse or child offer a hint of something greater than ourselves.

When we ignore our spirituality and therefore close off our receptivity, we will place limits on the love that others try to give us. We will pull away from love, not wishing to be smothered. Or we will demand more love, fearing that rejection is just around the corner and must be held at bay by constant reassurances from our partner that we are important. Either way we lose. We lose because we view receiving love as somehow making us vulnerable to future abandonment, so we anxiously seek more of it (reassurance and devotion) to feel safe, or we seek less of it (a need for personal space, a sense of independence, a belief that "I am my own person") to feel safe.

No wonder relationships are a confusing mess sometimes. We don't know what we want. We give love in waves, and we often give halfheartedly. Our ability to receive and give love to a partner, however strong, is still limited.

The Power of Spiritual Beliefs

Cynthia's only child died in a fall. The child was the love of her life and Cynthia was devastated. Little by little she tried to put the pieces of her life back together but found it almost impossible. Her soul ached. Fortunately, Cynthia had religious beliefs. They were understandably shaken after the death of her daughter—Cynthia could not understand why God allowed such a thing to happen—but she never lost her faith completely. I spoke to her one day.

"Cynthia," I said, "imagine that you had died first. Imagine that your daughter was left without you and that she was suffering. Do you believe that you would be able to watch her from heaven?"

"Yes," she said.

"And while you were watching her, would you want her to be suffering so much?"

"No, of course not. I would want her to remember me with love, but I would yell out a cheer in heaven the day I saw her playing happily."

"Is it possible," I said, "that your daughter wants the same for you?"

Cynthia used this insight to catapult her more profoundly toward God. Not only did she realize more vividly that her daughter was alive in heaven and watching her at that very moment, she realized that if she stayed devoted to God she would stay nearer to her daughter. "Because that's where my daughter is," she said. "With God."

The evidence that associates mental and physical health with a high level of spirituality is strong. It is impossible to say whether spirituality creates emotional and physical health, or whether healthy people are more likely to be religious, or if some other factor is at work.

Couples who pray together also report significantly more respect for each other, are more trusting, help each other out with household chores, and are more likely to agree on how to raise children.

Perhaps one of the reasons spiritual beliefs help people cope and heal is that such beliefs foster connections with others. A spiritual person is expected to be less self-focused and more other-focused. We expect such a person to be kind and considerate and forgiving. A famous study in California revealed that of people who died during a certain time frame, the best predictor of their mortality was not their health or eating habits but their social ties. People with fewer ties to others (who were unmarried, had few friends, did not attend church) died at a rate two to five times higher than people with strong social ties.

Researcher James Lynch reported that no disease kills people at the rate that loneliness does. For all races and both sexes, people under age seventy who were single, widowed, or divorced died at a rate that was up to ten times higher than married people.

In a study of Israeli soldiers, men who answered yes to the question "Does your wife show you her love?" were half as likely to develop heart disease years later.

Something about connecting meaningfully to others has life-promoting properties. We tap into a mystical dimension of human love. Is that dimension spiritual? Or can it ultimately be explained biologically?

I thought again of the old couple and the husband in the wheelchair. He was willing to sacrifice his desire to walk for the sake of his beloved wife. And she was willing to sacrifice her peace of mind by allowing him to struggle to walk.

Their love was not biological. It was spiritual.

22
no, I can't wait

"Would you hurry up?" Dave called out to his wife. He tapped the steering wheel impatiently while his wife Sharon was still rushing around inside the house.

"I'm coming, I'm coming!" she said on her way out the door.

"It's about time," Dave said. "You knew I wanted to get an early start for our trip. Now we'll hit some heavy traffic."

Sharon stayed quiet. There was nothing she could say that would appease her husband. She also felt a mixture of anger and guilt. Yes, she was late. Yes, she knew that Dave reminded her to be ready on time. But on the other hand, why did he make such a big deal out of it? What's an extra fifteen minutes? Shouldn't *she* be more important to him than arriving at some silly destination on time?

∾ patience: find joy in the small things

Some people look upon impatience as a virtue. An impatient person, it is sometimes thought, simply has high standards and is intolerant of mediocrity. But when Dave criticized his wife, Sharon, for running late, was that really virtuous? It wasn't if he put timeliness ahead of kindness or love. Dave was making a mistake of the soul. At that moment, he valued his wife only according to her usefulness.

But we shouldn't confuse patience with sluggishness or apathy. If Dave didn't care what time they left he might appear patient, but he would really be exhibiting indifference. Patience is not a ho-hum attitude toward life. A patient person can have, and should have, a zest for living.

Patience goes beyond tolerance. It is not merely a calm state of mind or an acceptance of a frustrating situation. It goes deeper. At its ultimate point, patience is the soulful recognition that we exist to do good, especially in our personal relationships. It is the pursuit of nonsoulful pleasures that leads to impatience, because they never fully satisfy.

Impatience happens when trust is diluted by doubt and when the self is more important than the soul.

When a person sees the bigger picture and tries to live out a soulful purpose, the small frustrations in life are not viewed as hassles or obstacles to happiness. Instead they are viewed as lessons of love and as opportunities to persevere. Impatient people give up far more quickly than patient people do. An impatient person may look as if he really cares about an outcome and may look as if he will persevere in his efforts. But impatient people often abandon their efforts when the going gets tough. Why? Because impatience is not just eagerness. Patient people can be eager for an outcome but are willing to tolerate the wait if need be. Impatient people cannot tolerate the wait because they are not 100 percent sure they are on the right track.

That is why true patience is an outgrowth of a trusting soul. For a person to possess patience, she must trust that she is on the right path toward her soul's purpose, or else she will always be impatient to varying degrees.

In a relationship such as a marriage, when physical wants, desires, and comforts can take precedence over soulful desires, people lose sight of their true purpose. They then become impatient for certain outcomes (more money, a bigger house, a better job, a younger-looking mate, and so forth) because what they are really seeking is validation from some external source that they are good enough, smart enough, lovable enough, or worthwhile enough.

Even Dave who is impatient because Sharon is running late is really saying "I'm not worthwhile." He just doesn't realize that. Instead, his message to Sharon is "*You're* not worthwhile" (because she is late). He is simply projecting his own fears onto her. Impatient people take things too personally. They think that setbacks are a personal affront. They do that because at the moment of frustration they have placed themselves at the center of the universe.

Impatience Within Relationships

Certainly the daily hassles of life can cause us to be unnecessarily impatient and abrupt with our mates. Nobody's perfect. But some people get mad over small things a lot of the time. It's a mistake that doesn't need to happen. They slam computers when the program freezes, they curse at other drivers on a busy highway, and they get annoyed when the pasta is overcooked. This kind of impatience cuts little slices into the people who have to put up with them. It makes others feel small. Someone with a lot of impatience is basically saying "Right now, I am important and you are not." They don't seem to care so much about the impact that their outbursts have on others. They only care—at least at that moment—about having things go their way.

People who live with chronically impatient people are worn out. Their days are spent having to put up with a partner who makes mountains out of molehills and finds fault over insignificant things. These relationships can succeed, but only if there are many positive and loving interactions in between all the frustrating ones. A common difficulty is that it is easy to lose patience with an impatient person. The impatient person sets the tone for the relationship. When you confront an impatient person, it would be nice to hear something such as, "I know that my impatience is annoying. Bear with me while I try to overcome it." But what you hear instead is an argument for why they have a right to be upset or irritable.

But even reasonably patient people can become anxious and impatient when they experience life's hardships. An unexpected job loss, a health scare, behavioral or emotional problems with the kids, a marital crisis—all of these can wear down one's patience. If the setback is temporary, there may be no lasting negative effects. But what if the trying times linger for months or longer? What if the outcome is very uncertain? Can you convince yourself that everything will work out in the end?

Patience means the most when answers are not forthcoming and a long wait is anticipated. When my wife was near her sixth month of pregnancy with our third child, a medical test indicated a problem. At first the doctor suspected our child might have Down's syndrome. Then further tests revealed a chromosomal abnormality. A piece of the baby's first chromosome had detached, turned upside down, and reattached itself. The chromosome looked deformed.

The genetic counselor tried to explain. "The chromosome contains genetic information. We are concerned that when a piece of the chromosome broke off, some genetic material may have been lost."

"Lost?"

"In other words, the baby might develop with certain things missing." But what things? Nobody knew. The science of genetic mapping had not progressed that far in 1990. Of course, there was also the chance that no genetic material would be lost. We were given a choice: Have an abortion or take our chances. My wife and I were scared, but we did not want an abortion. What had been an exciting time of expectation had turned topsy-turvy into an anxious time. We had once been prepared to wait patiently for our baby to arrive in three months. Now we were anxious and impatient. The hardest part was not knowing for sure what would happen.

But then a remarkable thing happened. It was remarkable in that it came quietly and unannounced, and completely transformed our anxiety into calmness and our impatience into patience. It was the realization that it made no difference whether our child would be born with some deformity or disease. Not surprisingly, the next three months were like any other last trimester. We were excited, looking forward to the birth, and rarely even thought about our baby's chromosome problem. We could be patient because we knew we were on the right track, willing to accept what God had in mind for us.

As a postscript, our daughter was born perfectly healthy and there is no indication ten years later of any problems.

Finding Patience

When problems in life or in relationships surface and they cannot be solved right away, patience is called for. Eight opportunities arise from taking a patient stance:

P   Prepare yourself for whatever might happen.

A   Accept the situation as it currently stands.

T   Trust that ultimately something good can emerge.

I   Inspire those around you.

E   Examine your strengths and weaknesses.

N   Nurture hope: All problems are temporary.

C   Comfort yourself.

E   Explore new possibilities and gain a new perspective.

PREPARE

While you are waiting to find out what happens (Will your relationship survive a crisis? Will your health return?), prepare for all possible outcomes. You may not want your relationship to fail, but you can help yourself by trying to imagine one or two ways you could cope better if it should happen. If your relationship does not survive, would you have regrets? Is there something you could do now that might reduce those regrets? Now is not the time to let other aspects of your life fall by the wayside. Try to keep up with your obligations as best you can. You can also prepare for the possibility that all will work out well. But you still may want to change some aspects of your relationship to avoid future problems. What things can you try to improve today that might help your relationship in the future?

ACCEPT

An acceptable situation is one you've committed yourself to dealing with. You don't have to like your situation, but you must accept it. Too often, people deny relationship problems and then scramble at the last minute to make repairs. Acceptance is not passive. It is a full recognition of the situation so that you can make improvements. You need to accept that there will be setbacks, and accept that some changes can only occur over time. When you accept your relationship difficulties, you are not condoning them or giving up. You are fighting *for* something positive, instead of fighting *against* something that has happened and cannot be changed. A man who says, "How could my wife tell me she loves me if she had an affair?" is thinking in black-and-white terms and is painting himself into a corner (he cannot trust she loves him because if she loved him she wouldn't have cheated). When that same man gets to the point where he asks, "What needs to happen for me to start believing—even a little bit—that she does indeed love me?" he is accepting (not fighting against) the fact that she had an affair, and is fighting *for* healthy progress.

TRUST

After you've done all you can, you have to develop a deeper trust. While you can wish for a certain outcome, it is helpful to trust that whatever the outcome it will ultimately be for the best. That is hard, especially when you truly believe that you know what is best. But it is a mistake to avoid the spiritual side of your situation. What you think is best may not always be best for your soul. Suffering and loss often seem unjust or meaningless. Even if you believe that some good can come from your loss (for example, Candy Lightner started Mothers Against Drunk Driving after her daughter was killed by a drunk driver), the loss itself may be irreplaceable. Still, you are likely to cope better with whatever happens if you can look for the good that can come out of it rather than the good that you lost. And keep in mind that many people go through relationship turmoil but years later believe that the experience was helpful, even fortunate.

INSPIRE

If you and your mate are going through a difficult time together, you can inspire one another by showing patience. (A casual, "don't worry about it" attitude is not what I mean. That attitude can actually make your partner impatient because it sounds like you are minimizing his or her concerns. A better way is to acknowledge that the concerns are legitimate but that you are trusting that all will work out with committed effort.) Often, a partner who is frustrated by their mate's ways wants immediate changes made. That attitude, while understandable, can be discouraging when some changes cannot be made overnight. When possible, telling your mate "I have faith in you" not only displays patience but also inspires him to want to change. If there is a financial or health problem, saying "We will get through this together" reveals a patient and optimistic outlook that will help your mate to feel the same way.

EXAMINE

During the times of relationship stress or crisis, your strong points and your weaknesses need to be examined. Now is the time to rely on one another for support, to ask for help, or to offer it when needed. Perhaps you are good at providing practical help (cooking meals, running errands) but not as adept at giving emotional support (being a good listener). You may be unable to improve your weaknesses right away, but you can become aware of them and resolve to make improvements in the future. If you are unsure what your strengths or weaknesses might be in the situation, ask your mate what he or she needs from you right now. Can you provide it?

NURTURE HOPE

All problems are temporary. Even if the outcome is not what you want and is permanent (the loss of a relationship, for example), the negative effects of that outcome are not permanent. Patience is easier to come by if you can nurture your belief that your problems are temporary.

COMFORT

Tolerating the wait is made easier when you can be comforted. Spend time with friends and family. (Be careful about soliciting advice. Everybody has an opinion and may advise you in ways that make you more confused or agitated.) Remind yourself of the many difficulties you've overcome in the past. Do what you can to find some peaceful time with your partner, even if you and he are at odds. Try to put aside some differences even for a little while and do something as a couple or as a family that might be enjoyable. When a couple is trying to fix problems in their relationship, they often get too serious. They stop having fun together. Everything they do gets put under a microscope and they cannot relax. But if you allow each other some time to make necessary changes, and if you offer comfort to one another during this time, you may discover you can handle the wait a little better.

EXPLORE

If the difficult times are severe enough, you won't look upon yourself or your partner quite the same way again. You may discover qualities—both flattering and unflattering—about each other. The more intense the problem, the more likely you cannot revert to your former style of relating once the problem is resolved. Talk to your mate about how your "new" relationship might look. Choose an image that is positive. A good question to explore: *What would I like my mate to understand about me right now that I don't think he or she fully understands?* Use this time as an opportunity to gain greater intimacy and understanding of one another.

Practicing patience on a daily basis is one way of showing love. When you allow impatience to grow, you whittle away devotion to your mate because *your* feelings and *your* needs start to take center stage.

23
why bother?

Your relationship—indeed, your very life—is like a boat on the ocean seeking the shore. It needs a direction and an ultimate destination, otherwise it is lost. Your direction in life is usually mapped out by focusing on predictable landmarks—education, job, love, kids, or perhaps an attempt at some remarkable achievement. You set those goals because you want to be happy. Ironically, Americans have more money, more luxuries, and more opportunities than ever before, but Americans are not any happier. In fact, rates of depression are predicted to be ten times higher in the next few years than they were just a few generations ago. Americans are lonelier and more detached from one another. Rates of childhood disorders such as attention deficit disorder have doubled and tripled in the past thirty years, coinciding with the precipitous decline in marriages and stable households.

Why aren't people happier? Why aren't relationships more satisfying? One reason is that the goals people set are often based on self-gratification instead of soul-gratification. People crave the sweets of life (success, money, sex) and a short time later they want more, never feeling fulfilled. Part of the problem is that people act in ways that diminish, rather than inspire, hope.

Hordes of single people under age thirty are choosing low-commitment relationships over marriage because they lack faith that marriages will work out.

They've even given up on romantic love and have chosen instead to make money and have fun, but at the expense of meaningful relationships. Sadly, they long for a marriage that will be fulfilling and even spiritual; they just don't trust it can really happen. (In one study of 800 college alumni, those who rated money and job success as more important than having good friends and a close marriage were twice as likely as their classmates to describe themselves as "fairly" or "very" unhappy.)

People don't trust that their future can be meaningful, so they grasp for whatever they can get now. But the things they grab for are not hopeful, meaningful, or soulful. They are meaningless. They are soulless.

Another problem is that while people seek vainly to find lasting happiness through pleasure, they miss out on discovering joy. Happiness is fleeting and subject to the whims of an arbitrary world. Joy goes deeper. People who are joyous may sometimes experience a hard life, but they do so with soft hearts and happy thoughts.

Joy is a by-product of having a meaningful life. You cannot be joyous and purposeless at the same time. Joyous people are able to see beyond the day-to-day frustrations and discover that their life is rich in meaning and purpose, regardless of adversity. (Mother Teresa was joyful. Yet on a daily basis she was faced with poverty, sickness, rampant disease, and personal sacrifice.)

Too many relationships lack purpose and are therefore either dead or dying. The couples simply go along day after day without a sense that their life together has any real meaning. They may wish for a brighter future—maybe marriages that will last or children who will make them proud—but they don't possess the real optimism that their life together will stand for something more than the accumulation of possessions and, if lucky, a retirement account that will allow for a comfortable lifestyle.

ೲ nurture optimism

As the song from the musical *Damn Yankees* proclaims, "You gotta have hope." Couples trying to make their relationship work can have a tough enough time these days, but their job is tougher when one of them is a pessimist by nature. Young adults whose parents divorced have a bleaker outlook on marriage. Are they simply realists using good, cautious judgment when they hesitate about marriage? Actually, their skepticism helps to create the very thing they hope to avoid—relationship failure. The more pessimistic one's outlook about the future success of a relationship, the more likely the following will occur:

- *Low commitment.* This increases the chances that devotion to one another will be lackluster.
- *Living together without marriage.* This tends to further reduce the importance of marriage in the minds of the cohabiting couple, and decreases the odds of relationship success.
- *Diminished perseverance when problems need fixing.* Pessimistic persons give up more quickly than optimists.
- *No goals or goals that lead only to superficial and fleeting satisfaction.*
- *Sabotaging the relationship.* Since negative outcomes are expected, pessimists sometimes provoke problems so they won't have to tolerate the wait.

In contrast, hopeful people persevere in their efforts to make their relationships wonderful and fulfilling. Hope is a yearning for good to happen, combined with a belief that it can happen. But how can a couple nurture hope when they have reason to feel hopeless? Or as one woman once told me, "My relationship isn't good, and I don't trust the man who says he'd like to marry me. If I simply hope for things to improve, won't I be tolerating something I shouldn't have to tolerate? Won't I be persisting in a mistake?"

There is a difference between someone who ignores signs of relationship disaster and maintains hope that all will be well (this person does not want to see the truth), and someone who sees clearly what the problems are and chooses to face them squarely with optimism. A misguided optimist is operating from fear. He or she fears losing a relationship and so maintains a cheery outlook and overlooks important information about his or her partner.

When hope is absent or in disrepair, people can become hopeful anyway, if they build the foundation upon which hope rests.

The Four Underpinnings of Hope

Jeanine was starting to feel hopeless. It had been six months since her fiancé had admitted he'd maintained a rather intimate but long-distance relationship on the Internet with a woman even after his relationship with Jeanine had begun. His "affair" was now over, that she believed. And Jim was apologetic. He admitted he had his reasons for doing what he did, but no good excuse. He was wrong, and he wanted Jeanine to trust him and to keep their wedding plans intact.

Jeanine wasn't at all sure she could accept what he did. She might be able to forgive him but not necessarily trust him enough to marry him. When I probed for other concerns, Jeanine realized that hope had been dashed in two areas: She lost hope that her relationship with Jim would work out, and she lost hope that she could trust her judgment in the future with other men. "Am I destined to remain single all my life?" she despaired.

Her friends and family tried to sound hopeful. Some told her that Jim was a jerk and she'd find a new man in no time. Others encouraged her to hang in there with Jim, convinced she'd feel better in another few months. Whatever the message, it was always upbeat. So why wasn't she brimming with hope? Because she never felt that her friends, however well intended they were, really listened to her. They wanted her to feel better, but they never went beyond sympathy to true understanding.

> *Before you can appreciate cheery advice and optimistic forecasts, you need to feel understood at a deeper level. Hope takes root not simply when someone is listening, but when you feel truly heard.*

The first underpinning to hope is formed when you *feel understood at a heartfelt level*. Actually, Jeanine did not think that Jim understood her pain at the level she needed. He was growing frustrated with her inability to put matters behind her and move forward. He'd say, "I'm sorry," but his underlying message was "You shouldn't be feeling the way you do anymore. Get over it." Had Jim been able to say, "I don't blame you for feeling the way you do. I know I'll never do anything to make you mistrust me ever again, but I also know you have a right to be skeptical," then Jeanine would know that her doubts and anxiety made sense to Jim. She would start to feel hopeful.

Jeanine's friends believed that she would find another man if her relationship with Jim ended. But by offering her quick reassurances they missed an opportunity to let her express her worries and arrive at an optimistic conclusion by herself. All they had to do was show her that they cared about her and that her worries were understandable—without jumping in to fix her. Often, that's all a person needs in order to sort through pain and arrive at a realistic conclusion.

A second underpinning to hope is *faith*. Faith is a willingness to trust despite uncertainties. If you have faith that your friends will never abandon you or that your spouse is devoted to you, then any relationship or personal problem won't make you feel hopeless. If you have faith that you have the resources needed to cope with a problem, you won't feel hopeless. This belief will get you through hard times.

Most of us think that *we* know what's best and have a difficult time relying on faith. But Jeanine was able to recall times in her life when what she'd thought were major disappointments turned out to be blessings in disguise. She wasn't sure if a breakup with Jim would be a blessing or not. But by nurturing her faith that whatever happened would turn out for the best—even when she didn't have all the answers—helped her to remain optimistic.

A third underpinning to hope is *committed work*. People who sit back and do nothing about their situation are dousing the fires of hope. But doing *anything* that gives them some degree of influence can spark their optimism. Doing something is always better than doing nothing. Active, committed work often leads to new ideas, which will also inspire hope. Couples trying to mend a relationship are usually out of sync with one another when it comes to committed work. Usually, one of them is more committed than the other. This leads to a herky-jerky pattern of progress that can be discouraging. Eventually, neither one is willing to work hard unless the other works hard. Their hope deteriorates and their anger rises.

Jeanine needed to work on sorting through her feelings to see if trust would ever again be possible. But Jim needed to commit himself to being as faithful and as reassuring to her as possible. Without each of them doing what was needed, they would feel less hopeful about their future.

The final underpinning to hope is *meaningfulness*. When one's life or marriage turns upside down and hope seems distant, the belief that one's life can still be meaningful despite loss, tragedy, or discouragement will instill hope. But that means you must learn to stop asking "Why?" ("Why did he do this to me?") and start asking "How?" ("How can I turn what happened into something positive or constructive?"). The answers may not come easily, but they need to come. For example, Jeanine's father had cheated on her mother and Jeanine had always been distant from her dad as a result. The crisis in her relationship with Jim made her realize that her inability to have a close connection with her father may have impeded her ability to objectively assess her situation with Jim.

Hope can arise from suffering when suffering serves a purpose. Sometimes the purpose is obvious, such as when you make a painful sacrifice for the sake of someone else. Parents who make financial sacrifices for their children's benefit hope that their sacrifice will pay off later, for example when one parent gives up their income to stay at home with the kids—or when a parent takes on a second job to defray the costs of college. But what if the purpose is not obvious? Many relationships undergo crises that are unasked for and seem unfair. When a husband comes home one night and unexpectedly tells his wife of twenty-five years he might not be in love with her anymore, how can she maintain hope? One way is to discover a meaning to the crisis.

But in order to inspire hope, the meaning that is provided must have healing qualities. For example, if the meaning offered was negative, such as "I'm worthless and unlovable and that is why he left me," then despair, not hope, will result. But trying to arrive at positive meaning for the negative events in one's life takes time. The search for meaning must necessarily take time when the loss or adversity was particularly profound. The search is an opportunity to correct distortions (saying "It's all my fault" is probably a distortion). Ultimately, you may never discover a good reason for why something bad happened. Why do innocent babies die? Why did the accident happen? Why did his heart give out at such a young age? Yet, meaning can emerge over time. One young couple could not understand why their one-year-old child had to die after many surgeries to try and correct a deformed heart. Two years later the mother was able to provide some meaning to her loss.

Suffering is bad enough. But the meanest form of suffering is suffering without meaning.

"I want desperately to see my baby again," she said. "While I don't understand why God let my child die, I do know that I am a more prayerful person since his death. I've come to believe more strongly in an afterlife. I believe my baby is happy in heaven and I believe that if I do my best to lead a good life, I will be with my baby forever some day. My child's life and death will be more meaningful to me if I choose to become a better person as a result. Otherwise, his death would have been entirely senseless."

She was able to make sense of her child's death in a way that was positive and meaningful. As a result, she had hope that she would some day be reunited with her son.

~

Suffering is inevitable if you love hard enough and live long enough. Then you have a choice: to shake a fist at the forces that allowed suffering, or to embrace all that has been good and glorious and loving and meaningful in your life. One choice is hopeful, the other hopeless. Which will you choose?

24

I'm sorry, you are not forgiven

"I just try to forget about it," Jake said. "People make mistakes and I know that Wendy is human and is entitled to make mistakes, too."

The mistake Jake is referring to was a one-night stand that Wendy had about four years earlier. The guy was her former boyfriend. He had been visiting the area, phoned Wendy, they met for coffee, and one thing led to another. Jake never would have found out about it except that Jake's brother just happened to see Wendy romantically kissing some guy in the parking lot of a diner. What made the situation worse was that Wendy and Jake were planning on getting married in three months. Jake was ready to call the whole thing off, but Wendy was able to persuade him that her fling did not mean she wasn't in love with him.

Four years and one child later, their marriage seems to be working. Jake says he has forgiven her. But has he? He still gets angry when he thinks about her betrayal. Does that mean he really hasn't forgiven? That's what Wendy thinks. When the two of them watched a movie where the plot involved an affair, Wendy noticed that Jake got sullen and standoffish. She didn't know whether to be angry with herself for having been so stupid four years ago, or to be angry with Jake for not letting go of the matter.

∾ absorb the pain for the sake of love

It is hard to forgive the deepest hurts. When a couple faces a severe crisis in their relationship and wants to reconcile, forgiveness is not optional. It's a necessity.

A person is not being stupid if he or she struggles when trying to forgive, or is so angry that forgiveness doesn't seem possible (at least now). Genuine forgiveness is a strenuous and time-consuming process. But it also has a soulful dimension. It is soulful because it requires that the victim absorb the pain and not retaliate, even when retaliation is justified.

You can forgive without reconciling, but you cannot reconcile without forgiving.

Some people withhold forgiveness so as to have a weapon ready for future combat. They want to hold it over their partner's head. Others choose not to forgive the smaller hurts that can happen in any relationship. Those hurts stack up and eventually impede relationship growth. Other people forgive too soon out of fear. Perhaps they fear losing the relationship or they wish to avoid conflict. But what they offer is not genuine forgiveness. These kinds of mistakes create more problems in the long run. In order to succeed at forgiving a serious offense, it is helpful to know exactly what forgiveness is and what it isn't. Otherwise, ignorance may complicate an already difficult process.

Dr. Robert Enright at the University of Wisconsin is a pioneer in the study of forgiveness. Through his efforts and those of his colleagues, the forgiveness process is not only better understood but has become part of the treatment plan for many therapists. He defines forgiveness as a willingness to abandon resentment and negative judgment toward the offending person (to which the injured person has a right), while fostering compassion and goodwill toward the offender (who does not deserve it). There are three key components to this definition. First, forgiveness begins as a *decision,* not a feeling. One must willfully choose to act forgiving even though one's emotions say otherwise. Second, it is an *abandonment of resentment.* People who stoke their anger despite a claim of forgiveness are choosing to remain bitter. Last, and most difficult of all, one must *show compassion* or goodwill (generosity, love, understanding, and so on) toward the offending person.

The Path of Forgiveness

Psychiatrist Richard Fitzgibbons points out that children often use denial to cope with pain or loss. As a result, many children carry unresolved anger with them into adulthood. For example, a person who felt abandoned by a parent after a divorce may pull away from a spouse or cling to a spouse as a way to cope with fears of rejection. Either way, it may be necessary to forgive one's parents before one can cleanly deal with a painful relationship issue.

We become better people when we forgive, and bitter people when we don't.

If you are struggling to forgive your partner, ask yourself: *Have I ever been hurt like this before?* If the answer is yes and if you still feel resentful over that injury, your ability to judge the current situation fairly may be compromised. A useful exercise is to sit quietly and imagine that the person who hurt you is in front of you. Repeat aloud the words *I forgive you* and pay close attention to the thoughts and feelings that emerge. Repeat the phrase at least ten times, each time noticing what thoughts or feelings come up for you. Chances are two things may happen. First, your anger may lessen as you repeat the phrase. Second, you will become aware of what issues are sticking points for you. For example, if after repeating the words *I forgive you* the thoughts that follow are *but only because I'm afraid of losing you,* you now have greater insight into issues you need to face.

Forgiveness isn't fair. The wrongdoer doesn't deserve forgiveness but is given it as a gift. The victim who forgives has no choice but to absorb the pain, to take the hit, to not hit back.

FORGIVENESS IS NOT . . .

Condoning. In fact, it is the opposite. You can only truly forgive an act that is recognized as being wrong.

Excusing. To excuse a behavior is to say that the wrongdoer couldn't help himself, or that he was under the influence of forces outside of himself. It is really a way of saying that the wrongdoer did nothing wrong. If there is a legitimate excuse, then forgiveness isn't necessary. But often the wrongdoer made a choice to act the way he did.

Forgetting. When the injustice is profound, it will always be remembered. It simply will cease to hold power over the victim once forgiveness happens.

A quick fix. Bringing flowers to your spouse and saying "Forgive me" might suffice for small infractions. But for larger hurts the process of forgiveness takes time. The wrongdoer should not accuse the victim of a moral lapse simply because the victim is finding it hard to forgive.

Tolerating the injustice. If the wrongdoer continues to harm you, you may need to end the relationship. Forgiveness is still possible, however.

A power play. If you lord it over the wrongdoer or "forgive" so as to make the other person perpetually indebted to you, you are keeping the other person in a one-down position. Forgiveness evens the playing field.

Some people feel they can forgive only after the wrongdoer has been punished. One woman was able to forgive her husband for cheating on her after he was involved in a near-fatal car accident. The desire to see the wrong-doer suffer is understandable. But retaliation as a prerequisite to forgiveness is not forgiveness. However, the wrongdoer should do all that he or she can to make amends. Making amends doesn't balance the scales; only forgiveness achieves that. But making amends is a sign that the offending person wants to reconcile and is truly sorry for what has happened.

The Phases of Forgiveness

Typically, people go through several predictable phases before they can finally forgive a deep hurt. If the offense is not too severe, forgiveness may come sooner.

PHASE ONE: UNCOVERING

This phase involves understanding the nature of the hurt. While this may seem easy, many people underreact or overreact and thereby distort the true nature of the offense. For example, when a person discovers that their partner has been lying to them about many things (such as their past, spending habits, and so forth), the full meaning of what has happened may not hit them immediately. Only later, when there has been time to think things through, might a person discover that they no longer trust their partner and that the entire relationship is now undermined. It is at this phase that people are likely to forgive falsely; to apply a quick fix so as not to have to examine their relationship too closely. It is also at this phase that the injured person eventually becomes more aware of his anger. At the beginning of this chapter, Jake had forgiven Wendy for her one-night stand. Initially, he was furious. He found himself imagining over and over Wendy having sex with another man.

At stage one, common thoughts include:

- *This is so unfair.*
- *How could he [she] do this to me?*
- *My life will never be the same again!*
- *This relationship will never be the same again!*

Psychiatrist and author Dr. Richard Fitzgibbons is an expert on anger and the forgiveness process. He notes that after a deep hurt, one's anger can be dealt with in only three ways. The first way is to deny one's anger, the second is to express anger either actively or passively, and the final way is to forgive. It is at this first phase of forgiveness that a person needs to examine how his or her anger is being dealt with. When the hurt is denied or if anger is expressed in an uncontrolled way, innocent bystanders often pay the price as anger with the offending person is sometimes displaced instead onto them.

PHASE TWO: DECISION

At this phase, a person considers forgiveness as an option. Usually, the person realizes that prior ways of coping with the offense have not really helped. Persons using denial are often uncomfortable expressing anger openly. They find the idea of forgiveness appealing since it can allow them to deal with their hurt without necessarily venting anger. People who vent their anger often discover over time that their anger is not diminishing and that it is now contributing further to the decline of the relationship. Forgiveness then seems a potentially worthwhile option. In phase two, it helps when people learn what forgiveness is and is not, otherwise misunderstandings will impede the healing process. It is at the end of phase two that a person decides more strongly to forgive, even though it also may seem impossible to achieve.

Common thoughts during this phase include:

- *I want to overcome my anger, but forgiveness doesn't seem fair.*
- *I know forgiveness is the right thing to do, but I don't feel like forgiving.*
- *In my head I forgive, but my heart wants revenge.*
- *I'd rather not think about what happened, but I know that ignoring what happened won't help me to forgive.*

PHASE THREE: WORK

In the work phase, the injured person focuses less on herself and more on developing empathy or compassion for the offending person. This is accomplished by

In phase three, the injured person must absorb the pain rather than pass it on to the offender or to other innocent parties. In other words, the injured person chooses to act morally rather than with vengeance.

trying to better understand the offender's personal history so as to view him in a broader, more benevolent light. This is not done to make excuses for the hurtful actions. The offending person chose to act the way he did, and his actions are not to be excused. However, the better an understanding one has of a person's background or of the factors that led to the offense, the easier it can be to view him less harshly.

Anger can still be strong at this phase, according to Dr. Fitzgibbons, but the injured person realizes that anger is also a defense against feelings of inadequacy and the fear of future betrayal. Efforts to improve self-esteem and reduce the likelihood of future betrayal can help here. If the offending partner is truly sorry, this phase can be a bit easier, especially if that person makes sincere attempts to change.

Common thoughts at phase three include:

- *What he did was terribly wrong, but there were many times he showed me love.*
- *I didn't deserve this. But she didn't deserve many of the things that happened to her, either.*
- *I'm trying to put myself in his shoes so as to understand why he did what he did.*
- *I realize that there is no way he can fully make amends or make up for what he did to me. I'll have to forgive him.*

PHASE FOUR: DEEPENING

Here, the injured party notices an increase in feelings of love and trust and a greater ability to control anger. This is also a phase where the meaning to one's loss or injury can be discovered. Some couples realize that the injury and subsequent forgiveness propelled them to a higher relationship level. Some realize that old, unresolved issues with their family had been blocking their efforts to have a successful relationship. Many realize that they, too, have needed to be forgiven in the past and that they are just as weak as their partner is at times. Often, life takes on a new purpose as a couple unites to overcome their hurt and strengthen their relationship. In this deepening phase, the remnants of hurt and anger and mistrust may linger, but they no longer sting.

Common thoughts at this phase include:

- *What happened was wrong, but I have learned something from it.*
- *I wouldn't want what happened to me to happen again, but in some ways I am a better person for having endured it.*
- *Even though I have forgiven, I still notice the pain emerging once in a while.*
- *Many people have had to experience what I experienced, and they made it through.*

You can choose to latch on to memories of betrayal and become fearful and bitter, or you can latch on to hope while remembering that which has been good and loving in your life. The soul can go either way, toward good or away from it. You have to bend your will and point your soul in the right direction.

25
I don't know
how to sacrifice

Ted has been married for ten years and has three children. In therapy, he revealed that his wife is a good woman and a wonderful, devoted mother. But she is boring. She has no interest in learning new things or traveling to exotic places, or even going to a movie once in a while. His intent is to leave her because he wants to be more fulfilled. He feels that he deserves a more challenging, exciting life. He has paid his dues, he says. He has also fallen in love with another woman, someone who shares his romantic vision for the future.

No one debates his right to do what he wants. He has free choice. But *should* he do what he is planning? Or doesn't he have a right to happiness when life, after all, is so short? The answer lies not so much with values but with virtues. Today, virtues have been tossed aside from discussions of human behavior when they collide with "rights." But people need to know they are making a mistake of the soul when *personal* rights take precedence over what *is* right.

Everyone has values. But everyone's values are not virtuous. Modern society embraces a kind of moral relativism. If something works for me, it is good. If it doesn't work for me, it is not good and can be abandoned. When relationships are weighed according to relativistic standards, they are judged—sadly—by their usefulness rather than their soulfulness.

Ted's marriage is no longer useful, and now he wants out.

ꙮ discover the sacred purpose to your relationship

What if you believed that your marriage was sacred? What would you do differently?

Such a belief could send your relationship soaring. But I suspect it would make you uncomfortable, too. To believe in the sacredness of marriage means that marriage has the potential to not only make you happy but holy. That's quite an obligation. It would mean that the vow "for better or worse" would have to be taken seriously by each, as would the vow "to love and cherish." But many couples don't walk the road of sacredness once they get married. They walk—slowly at first, but inevitably—down the road of selfishness. They insist on being loved more than they show love, of receiving more than they give. And sacrifice is looked upon as unfair, not part of the original bargain.

When love is sacred, the sacrifices we make for the beloved other do not feel like sacrifices. Yes, on some days we may be tired and grouchy and not feel like doing much of anything for those we love. But when real sacrifices are called for and love is sacred, we say things like "It is the least I can do," and we mean it. Yet, when love is not sacred, when our relationship is built on the value of usefulness—of me-first-ness—sacrifice becomes a burden. We resent it and deep down we feel owed. Similarly, when love is romantic only (fun but lacking depth), any sacrifices made eventually become wearisome. If too much sacrifice is necessary, even the romantic relationship loses its appeal. "It's not worth it," we say. But when love is sacred, it is always worth it.

Romantic love is exciting stuff. It fills the heart, the mind, and the body, but not the soul.

But is it possible that your relationship could be sacred, even if you are not married? If you look around at the quality of other people's relationships, there are many couples who live together, unmarried, who treat each other with a love and respect that many married couples have not achieved. The sacred aspect is, at least in part, what the couple puts into the relationship. They help make it sacred as a result of their virtuous actions.

But sacredness also requires something outside the realm of the couple. The soulful qualities that make up a deeply sacred relationship have the potential to be completely met only within marriage, no matter how hard an unmarried couple tries. If you think of sacredness as a vessel into which a couple pours itself, an unmarried couple pours itself into a smaller vessel. They may fill it, but there is a limit. In marriage, the vessel is ever-expanding.

A married couple who despises one another pours little that is good into the vessel, compared to a very loving but unmarried couple. But a married couple, devoted to one another and who believe in the sacredness of marriage, can pour themselves into their vessel and reach heights and depths well beyond other couples. That is because marriage is meant to be not just a physical union but a spiritual union—a union that is greater than the sum of its parts.

Does this sound biased? Does it sound unfair to nonspiritual couples? The truth is that the virtues most prized in life and in marriage are these: love, faith, hope, and charity. These virtues are spiritual. They are abstract, intangible, yet we all have felt them and understand how life-changing they can be when we experience them as fully as possible. A married couple has the *opportunity,* though it is not a sure bet, to reach spiritual heights by practicing these virtues. They can fully immerse themselves in the sacred. An uncommitted couple can step into shallow waters only and experience some of the sacredness, but never to a full depth. Why not? Because choosing to not commit fully to one another places limits on love. The couple promises to stay with one another, not until death do they part, but until they change their mind.

Determining What Is Morally Right

People have a fundamental choice in life and in their relationships: They can either adjust their lives according to a set of moral standards, or they can readjust the standards to fit their lives. Many of us choose the latter. We act the way we want to act, and then create a value to justify it.

Today, in the name of tolerance, wrong behavior is accepted as morally feasible. In fact, in some circles it isn't even wrong. Ironically, what is not tolerated today is *truth.* Truth has become relative. What's true for me is not necessarily true for you. Therefore, no one can be judged because there is no acceptable standard for moral action. But if there is no such thing as ultimate truth, it cannot—by definition—exist.

It isn't difficult to define which rules to live by. Moral dilemmas ("Is having sex okay when we've only recently met?" "Should I stay with him for the children's sake?") often arise not because of a clash in universal truths, but because of a clash between what we *want* to do and what we know we *ought* to do. It is true that some people with severe character deficits do not seem to have a conscience. But most of us do possess a conscience to varying degrees. As often as we are tempted to do the wrong thing in situations, we are tempted and urged to do the right thing by our conscience. For example:

- We know (or sense) instinctively that kindness is better than cruelty.
- We know that optimism feels better and leads to success more than pessimism does.
- We know that honesty is usually the best policy, certainly where personal relationships are concerned.
- We know that faithfulness and commitment do more to serve us in the long run than does unfaithfulness.
- After an argument, we know that the right thing to do is go to our partner and say that we feel badly for what happened and want to work things out.
- We know we should act in ways that bring out the best in our partners, not the worst.
- We know that intense striving for material gain makes us lose sight of those we love.
- We know that sincere gratitude, even for the small things, makes us feel happier.
- We know that a divine force is tugging at us, and we yearn for a life based on love, not greed or selfishness.

We know—or at least we sense—all of these things. And most of us would agree they are worthwhile goals. But still it is our human nature to take the paved road rather than the dirt path. We do all the right things until it starts to become inconvenient. Then we pull back and convince ourselves we've done enough when we've only done what was easy. It's easy to show love to a spouse when she is kind and responsive to your needs and wants. It's easy to be good-hearted and generous when the sun is shining and the bank account is overflowing.

The hard thing is to act with love when you have been betrayed or when you are overwhelmed with stress or unexpected loss. That is where a sense of sacrifice must come in. But when you love enough to sacrifice, when you love enough to suffer for the sake of the beloved other—as you do when you work a second job to pay a child's school expenses, or when you struggle to forgive a spouse who has betrayed you—you are doing the work of soul-building. Souls develop through the grit of pure love, and pure love is sacrificial and devotional, not just sunshine and flowers. Marriage, and involvement in any committed relationship, pushes you to make sacrifices, not once or twice, but repeatedly. This is not hardship, it is simply the consequence of love.

What If You Believed That Your Marriage Was Sacred?

In order to have strong moral character and a high sense of virtue, two things must occur: We must know the truth about what is right and what is wrong, and we must exercise our free will and choose what is right.

Choosing to act in any way we wish without worrying if it is right or wrong is not moral. Doing the moral thing but only because we are forced to or because we think someone is watching says little about our strength of character.

Often, doing the right thing seems to place limits on our freedom; it cramps our style. But the opposite is true: Choosing to act in ways that go against moral truth imprisons us, while doing what's right is freeing.

When we repeatedly choose to do the wrong thing, our bad habits become entrenched. Then we do more and more of those things and eventually some bigger things. Ultimately, we lose sight of the fact that we are even choosing wrong over right and our imprisonment goes on uninterrupted. One example is when a parent raises a child but still acts in a manner that places distance between himself and his child. Maybe he spends all his free time on recreation but not with his child. Maybe he criticizes his child much more than he ever praises. Over time, that parent may be unaware of how disconnected he has become. He may even convince himself he is a devoted father because he works so hard. Once he is made aware of his mistakes he may resent having to change because he has truly lost some of his moral vision. He thought he was doing the right things all along. Making changes then feels awkward and unfair, perhaps a bit confining. What he doesn't see is that he is more confined by his blindness to truth than he would ever be by an attempt to commit to truth. If he does not change, he will confine himself to a permanent relationship with his child that lacks vigor and deep devotion. Chances are that his wife will also resent his ways. She may even get closer to her child to compensate for her husband and in the process move further away from her husband emotionally.

If you believed your marriage was sacred, you would endeavor first to *know* and then to *do* the right things. Probably the first thing you would do differently is you would not take your marriage or your partner for granted. There is a story that was circulated shortly after the death of Mother Teresa. Mother Teresa was known worldwide for her sacrificial devotion to the poor and the dying on the streets of Calcutta, India. Once when she was visiting New York City, a wealthy businessman had an opportunity to meet her. Impressed by Mother Teresa's work, he opened his checkbook and asked her how much money she needed for the local convent. She declined his offer. He persisted and suggested perhaps that the Sisters might benefit from having a new van. Mother Teresa told him that instead he should go home and spend time with his family, and possibly volunteer some service at a soup kitchen. It was Mother Teresa's philosophy that charity began at home. Kindness to strangers was not as meaningful unless love and kindness was thriving at home.

If you believed your marriage was sacred:

- You would view the ups and downs of the relationship as an opportunity to persevere while trusting that faith would guide you.
- You would practice humility. Humility is not passivity or meekness. It is a recognition that you can learn so much from others, even others who seem to be less educated or less moral than yourself. A humble spouse will point out problems but in a way that shows love and respect to his or her partner. A humble spouse is grateful for all the little things many people take for granted.
- You would commit yourself not only to your partner's physical well-being but also to her spiritual well-being.
- You would forgive when necessary, and pray for the strength to forgive when forgiveness seems impossible.
- You would search for meaning during adversity. You would believe that there is a plan for your marriage that is for the good—despite hardship— and you would seek to uncover that plan and live it.
- You would have hope that your marriage will provide inspiration not just for your family, but for people whom you haven't even met yet.

- You would never rest on your laurels. You would want to be the best spouse and parent you can be at ages fifty, sixty, seventy, and so on until you die.
- You might feel very sad, but you wouldn't despair; you might feel angry but never bitter; you might feel guilty but never discouraged.
- You would trust, even when your own efforts to make matters right keep going wrong.

If you overlook the soul of your marriage, you overlook the very thing that can make your marriage joyful. When you view your marriage as sacred, you are not so likely to interpret fluctuations in feelings of love as reasons to question the validity of your relationship. Instead, you will endeavor to correct whatever changes may be necessary in your marriage as you operate on faith that your love, despite ups and downs, is genuine. And you will operate filled with hope that the relationship will continue to grow.

references

1

Brown, S., and A. Booth. "Cohabitation versus marriage: A comparison of relationship quality." *Journal of Marriage and the Family* 58 (1996): 668–678.

Forste, R., and K. Tanfer. "Sexual exclusivity among dating, cohabiting, and married women." *Journal of Marriage and the Family* 58 (1996): 33–47.

Moore, Kristin, and Thomas Steif. "Changes in marriage and fertility behavior: Behavior versus attitude in young adults." *Youth and Society* 22 (1991): 362–386.

Nock, Steven. "Comparison of marriages and cohabiting relationships." *Journal of Family Issues* 16 (1995): 53–76.

Stanton, Glenn. *Why Marriage Matters: Reasons to Believe in Marriage in Postmodern Society.* Colorado Springs, Colo.: Pinon Press, 1997, pp. 56–60.

Wu, Zheng. "Premarital cohabitation and postmarital cohabiting union formation." *Journal of Family Issues* 16 (1995): 212–232.

2

Bradbury, T., and F. Fincham. "Attribution and behavior in marital interactions." *Journal of Personality and Social Psychology* 63 (1992): 613–628.

Murray, S., J. Holmes, and D. Griffin. "The benefits of positive illusion: Idealization and the construction of satisfaction in close relationships." *Journal of Personality and Social Psychology* 70 (1996): 79–98.

4

Coleman, Paul. *Getting to the Heart of the Matter: How to Resolve Ongoing Arguments in Your Marriage Once and for All.* Holbrook, Mass.: Bob Adams, 1992.

5

Coleman, Paul. *The 30 Secrets of Happily Married Couples.* Holbrook, Mass.: Bob Adams, 1992.

Frank, E., C. Anderson, and D. Rubinstein. "Frequency of sexual dysfunction in 'normal' couples." *New England Journal of Medicine* 299 (1978): 111–115.

Greeley, Andrew. *Faithful Attraction: Discovering Intimacy, Love, and Fidelity in American Marriage.* New York: Tor, 1991, pp. 80, 119–120.

Hawton, K., D., Gath, and A. Day. "Sexual functioning in a community sample of middle-aged women and their partners." *Archives of Sexual Behavior* 23 (1994): 375–395.

Leitenberg, H., and K. Henning. "Sexual fantasies." *Psychological Bulletin* 117 (1995): 469–496.

O'Sullivan, L., and E. Allgeier. "Feigning sexual desire: Consenting to unwanted sexual activity in heterosexual dating relationships." *Journal of Sex Research* 35 (1994): 234–243.

Seidman, S., and R. Reider. "A review of sexual behavior in the United States." *American Journal of Psychiatry* 151 (1994): 330–341.

6

Coleman, Paul. *Getting to the Heart of the Matter: How to Resolve Ongoing Arguments in Your Marriage Once and for All.* Holbrook, Mass.: Bob Adams, 1992.

Gottman, J., C. Notarius, J. Gonso, and H. Markman. *A Couple's Guide to Communication.* Champaign, Ill.: Research Press, 1976, pp. 83–104.

7

Amato, P., and B. Keith. "Parental divorce and the well-being of children: A meta-analysis." *Psychological Bulletin* 110 (1991): 26–46.

Grych, J., and F. Fincham. "Interventions for children of divorce." *Psychological Bulletin* 111 (1992): 434–454.

Morrison, D., and M. Corro. "Parental conflict and marital disruption: Do children benefit when high-conflict marriages are dissolved?" *Journal of Marriage and the Family* 61 (1999): 626–637.

Stanton, Glenn T. *Why Marriage Matters: Reasons to Believe in Marriage in Postmodern Society.* Colorado Springs, Colo.: Pinon Press, 1997, p. 144.

Tein, J.Y., I. Sandler, and A. Zautra. "Stressful life events, psychological distress, coping, and parenting of divorced mothers: A longitudinal study." *Journal of Family Psychology* 14 (2000): 27–41.

Tucker, Joan, et al. "Parental divorce: Effects of individual behavior and longevity." *Journal of Personality and Social Psychology* 73 (1997): 381–391.

Wallerstein, J., and J. Lewis. "The long-term impact of divorce on children: A first report from a 25-year study." *Family and Conciliation Courts Review* 36 (1998): 368–383.

Whiteside, M., and B. Becker. "Parenting factors and the young child's post-divorce adjustment: A meta-analysis with implications for parenting arrangements." *Journal of Family Psychology* 14 (2000): 5–26.

Zill, N., D. Morrison, and M. Corro. "Long-term effects of parental divorce on parent-child relationships, adjustment, and achievement in young adulthood." *Journal of Family Psychology* 7 (1993): 91–103.

8

Almeida, D., J. Maggs, and N. Galambos. "Wives' employment hours and spousal participation in family work." *Journal of Family Psychology* 7 (1993): 233–244.

Biernat, M., and C. Wortman. "Sharing of home responsibilities between professionally employed women and their husbands." *Journal of Personality and Social Psychology* 60 (1991): 844–860.

Coleman, Paul. *How to Say It to Your Kids!* Paramus, N.J.: Prentice Hall, 2000, p. 146.

Hyde, J., J. DeLamater, and E. Hewitt. "Sexuality and the dual earner couple: Multiple roles and sexual functioning." *Journal of Family Psychology* 12 (1998): 354–368.

Shelton, B., and D. John. "Does marital status make a difference? Housework among married and cohabiting men and women." *Journal of Family Issues* 14 (1993): 401–420.

Strazdins, L., R. Galligan, and E. Scannell. "Gender depressive symptoms: Parents' sharing of instrumental and expressive tasks when their children are young." *Journal of Family Psychology* 11 (1997): 222–233.

Zuo, J. "The reciprocal relationship between marital interaction and marital happiness: A three wave study." *Journal of Marriage and the Family* 54 (1992): 870–878.

9

Coleman, Paul. "Cherish is the word I use to describe . . ." *Marriage* (March/April 2000): 52–53.

10

Buss, David. *Dangerous Passion.* New York: Free Press, 2000.

Goleman, D. "Analyzed: Mental Disorders or Normal Growth?" *New York Times,* 17 May 1988, p. 19.

11

Cohen, L., and R. Shotland. "Timing of first sexual intercourse in relationships." *Journal of Sex Research* 33 (1996): 291–299.

Hynie, M., J. Lydon, and A. Taradash. "Commitment, intimacy, and women's perception of premarital sex and contraceptive readiness." *Psychology of Women Quarterly* 21 (1997): 447–464.

Item printed in *New Woman* (October 1997): 61.

Laumann, E., J. Gagnon, R. Michael, and S. Michaels. *The Social Organization of Sexuality: Sexual Practices in the United States.* Chicago: University of Chicago Press, 1994, pp. 240, 507.

12

Christenson, A., and C. Heavey. "Gender and social structure in the demand/withdraw pattern of marital conflict." *Journal of Personality and Social Psychology* 59 (1990): 73–81.

Gottman, John. *Why Marriages Succeed or Fail.* New York: Simon & Schuster, 1994.

Notarius, Clifford, and Howard Markman. *We Can Work It Out: Making Sense of Marital Conflict.* New York: G.P. Putnam's Sons, 1993.

13

Gottman, John. *Marital Interactions: Experimental Investigations.* New York: Academic Press, 1979.

Margolin, G., and B. Wampold. "Sequential analysis of conflict and accord in distressed and nondistressed marital partners." *Journal of Consulting and Clinical Psychology* 49 (1981): 554–567.

14

Adams, J., and W. Jones. "The conceptualization of marital commitment: An integrative analysis." *Journal of Personality and Social Psychology* 72 (1997): 1177–1196.

Ferrell, David. "Characteristics of long-term first marriages." *Journal of Mental Health Counseling* 15 (1993): 446–460.

White, Lynn. "Determinants of divorce: A review." *Journal of Marriage and the Family* 52 (1990): 904–912.

15

Cooper, A., C. Scherer, S. Boles, and B. Gordon. "Sexuality on the Internet: From sexual expression to pathological expression." *Professional Psychology, Research, and Practice* 30 (1999): 154–164.

Gagnon, J., R. Michael, E. Laumann, and G. Kolata. *Sex in America: A Definitive Survey.* Boston: Little Brown, 1994.

Laumann, E., J. Gagnon, R. Michael, and S. Michaels. *The Social Organization of Sexuality: Sexual Practices in the United States.* Chicago: University of Chicago Press, 1994, p. 214.

16

Hazen, C., and P. Shaver. "Love and work: An attachment-theoretical perspective." *Journal of Personality and Social Psychology* 59 (1990): 270–280.

17

Christensen, A., and N. Jacobson. *Reconcilable Differences.* New York: Guilford, 2000.

Cordova, James, and Neil Jacobson. "Acceptance in couple therapy and its implications for the treatment of depression." In *Satisfaction in Close Relationships*, edited by Robert Sternberg and Mahzed Hojjat, 307–334. New York: Guilford, 1997.

19

Guerin, P., T. Fogarty, L. Fay, and J. Kautto. *Working with Relationship Triangles: The One-Two-Three of Psychotherapy.* New York: Guilford, 1996.

20

Pennebaker, James. *Opening Up: The Healing Power of Confiding in Others.* New York: Morrow, 1990.

21

Berkman, L., and S. Syme. "Social networks, host resistance, and mortality: A nine-year follow-up study of Alameda County residents." *American Journal of Epidemiology* 109 (1979): 186–204.

Greeley, Andrew. *Faithful Attraction: Discovering Intimacy, Love, and Fidelity in American Marriage.* New York: Tor, 1991.

Keenan, Paul. *Good News for Bad Days: Living a Soulful Life.* New York: Warner, 1998.

Koenig, Harold. *Is Religion Good for Your Health? The Effects of Religion on Physical And Mental Health.* New York: Haworth Pastoral Press, 1997.

Lynch, James. "The Broken Heart: The Psychobiology of Human Contact." In *The Healing Brain,* edited by Robert Ornstein and Charles Swencionis. New York: Guilford, 1990.

Medalie, J., and H. Goldbourt. "Angina pectoris among 10,000 men: Psychosocial and other risk factors as evidenced by a multivariate analysis of a five-year incidence study." *American Journal of Medicine* 60 (1976): 910–921.

West, Christopher. "A great 'nuptial mystery.'" *Inside the Vatican* (1999): 70–73.

23

Coleman, Paul. *Life's Parachutes: How to Land on Your Feet During Trying Times.* New York: Dell, 1993.

Myers, David. "The funds, faith, and friends of happy people." *American Psychologist* 55 (2000): 56–67.

Perkins, H. "Religious Commitment: Yuppie values and well-being in post-collegiate life." *Review of Religious Research* 32 (1991): 244–251.

24

Enright, R., S. Freedman, and J. Rique. "The psychology of interpersonal forgiveness." In *Exploring Forgiveness,* edited by R. Enright and J. North, 46–62. Madison Wisconsin: University of Wisconsin Press, 1998.

Fitzgibbons, R. "Anger and the healing power of forgiveness: A psychiatrist's view." In *Exploring Forgiveness,* edited by R. Enright and J. North, 63–74. Madison Wisconsin: University of Wisconsin Press, 1998.

index